JESUS

A Study on the Words of Matthew, Mark, Luke, and John

David R. Steele
Diane L. Bahn

CONCORDIA PUBLISHING HOUSE · SAINT LOUIS

24 LESSONS — STUDENT GUIDE

Published by Concordia Publishing House
3558 S. Jefferson Avenue, St. Louis, MO 63118-3968
1-800-325-3040 • cph.org

Manufactured in the United States of America

Library of Congress Cataloging-in-Publication Data

Names: Steele, David R. (Pastor) author. | Bahn, Diane L., author.
Title: Jesus: a study on the words of Matthew, Mark, Luke and John : leader guide / David R. Steele, Diane L. Bahn.
Description: Saint Louis : Concordia Publishing House, [2020] | Includes index.
Identifiers: LCCN 2019051777 (print) | LCCN 2019051778 (ebook) | ISBN 9780758663023 (paperback) | ISBN 9780758663030 (ebook)
Subjects: LCSH: Bible. Gospels—Study and teaching. | Jesus—Biography—Study and teaching.
Classification: LCC BS2556 .S65 2020 (print) | LCC BS2556 (ebook) | DDC 226.0071—dc23
LC record available at h8ps://lccn.loc.gov/2019051777
LC ebook record available at h8ps://lccn.loc.gov/2019051778

---

5 6 7 8 9 10 11 30 29 28 27 26

CONTENTS

Acknowledgments

This study of the Gospels grew out of love for the Scriptures by many people at St. John Lutheran Church, our home church where Diane and I wrote the lessons and taught them in our adult Sunday School class. First and foremost, I thank Diane Bahn, my teaching partner, whose knowledge of the Bible and ability to express its truths never cease to impress and humble me. I am also grateful for the encouragement of Martha Warnasch, Barbara Eldridge, Shirley Willingham, and Chris Leach. These godly women have a wonderful walk with Christ and are quick to praise God in any circumstance. They have been an inspiration for me in every class we have shared over the past ten years. Chris tirelessly edited the many drafts of the manuscript; thank you for sharing your editorial gifts! I thank Pastor David Bahn for editing the study for theological content despite his busy schedule. I am especially thankful for his wonderful gift of friendship. We thank the staff at Concordia Publishing House, particularly Rev. Wayne Palmer and Laura Lane, whose guidance has made this publication possible.

Foreword

The twenty-four lessons selected for this study come from all four Gospels and are arranged in the sequential order of Matthew. The four Gospel writers record about 270 events, miracles, and teachings from Jesus' life, yet aside from Jesus' resurrection, only one of His miracles is common to all four: the feeding of the five thousand. The twenty-four lessons begin with John's bold and clear statement of the deity of Jesus—He is the Word of God, who was with God, and who was God from the beginning. The study ends with Jesus' ascension and His Great Commission to all who would be His disciples.

Familiar events of Jesus' life are included in the twenty-four lessons. These include Jesus' miraculous birth, temptation in the wilderness, the calling of the disciples, the triumphal entry into Jerusalem, the crucifixion, resurrection, and ascension. The lessons also include the great themes of Jesus' ministry—His healing ministry, His great sermons and parables, His miracles demonstrating His lordship over His creation, and His teachings about the sacraments and prayer.

Each lesson is a stand-alone study that is not dependent on the previous lessons so that guests and visitors will feel comfortable joining your class in mid-stream. Lessons are designed to be completed in an hour with opening and closing prayers. We encourage participants to join in the opening prayer with whatever prayer requests and thanksgivings they have on their hearts. The closing prayer is a blessing on the class for the week to come.

The leader guide includes extensive notes to help the leader prepare for the class. Many of the examples come from our own personal experience, so the leader can feel comfortable drawing from his or her own experience. You will find there is too much material rather than too little. Summary and application questions are generally at the end of the lesson. You can focus on those if time runs short. Another helpful strategy to facilitate the discussion is to hand out the lessons a week in advance so that class participants can use the study as their devotional during the week.

A twenty-four-week-long Bible study may sound like a long time; it is certainly contrary to modern studies that change the topic every six to twelve weeks. But you will find that the study of Jesus' life and ministry will not grow wearisome. If you do have time constraints, a good survey of Jesus' life could also be done in twelve weeks using Lessons 1, 3, 4, 6, 10, 12, 14, 15, 17, 20, 22, and 23. Whichever study you decide to undertake, we pray that God richly blesses you with His peace and abundant blessings.

Christ, the Word

In the beginning was the Word,
and the Word was with God,
and the Word was God. *(John 1:1)*

Prayers

____

____

____

____

____

Background

The Holy Spirit guided each Gospel writer to direct his account to a different Christian group with a different point of emphasis:

Matthew wrote to a Jewish community. Also known as Levi, this tax collector was one of Jesus' twelve disciples. Matthew begins with Jesus' genealogy, showing He is in the line of David. This first Gospel includes the most references to Old Testament prophecies and the largest number of miracles to demonstrate to Jewish readers that Jesus is the Messiah.

Mark wrote to Gentiles, most likely Romans. The second Gospel is attributed to John Mark, a close associate of Peter in Rome who probably acted as Peter's secretary. Mark begins with John the Baptist, who fulfilled Old Testament prophecy by calling Israel to repentance to receive their Messiah. Mark is the shortest Gospel, and many scholars believe it was written first.

Luke wrote to Gentiles (Greeks) and places the birth of Jesus in the historical context of the Roman world. Luke was a physician and companion of Paul who traveled with him on many of his missionary journeys recorded in Acts. He carefully investigated the life of Christ from eyewitnesses to write an orderly account of the Gospel to make his benefactor, Theophilus, certain of all the things he had been taught about Jesus. He wrote both the Gospel of Luke and the Book of Acts.

John begins his Gospel at the moment of creation, giving us a glimpse into eternity where Jesus dwells in glory with the Father. John was one of Jesus' twelve disciples. His Gospel focuses on the deity of Jesus as the Son of God, His role in creating the universe, and His union with God the Father. John provides unique insights in Jesus' Jerusalem ministry and His final hours before the crucifixion.

Read John 1:1–18—The Word Became Flesh.

> 1 In the beginning was the Word, and the Word was with God,
> and the Word was God. 2 He was in the beginning with God. 3 All
> things were made through Him, and without Him was not any
> thing made that was made. 4 In Him was life, and the life was the
> light of men. 5 The light shines in the darkness, and the darkness
> has not overcome it.
>
> 6 There was a man sent from God, whose name was John. 7 He
> came as a witness, to bear witness about the light, that all might
> believe through him. 8 He was not the light, but came to bear wit-
> ness about the light.
>
> 9 The true light, which gives light to everyone, was coming into the
> world. 10 He was in the world, and the world was made through
> Him, yet the world did not know Him. 11 He came to His own, and
> His own people did not receive Him. 12 But to all who did receive
> Him, who believed in His name, He gave the right to become chil-
> dren of God, 13 who were born, not of blood nor of the will of the
> flesh nor of the will of man, but of God.
>
> 14 And the Word became flesh and dwelt among us, and we have
> seen His glory, glory as of the only Son from the Father, full of
> grace and truth. 15 (John bore witness about Him, and cried out,
> "This was He of whom I said, 'He who comes after me ranks be-
> fore me, because He was before me.'") 16 For from His fullness
> we have all received, grace upon grace. 17 For the law was given
> through Moses; grace and truth came through Jesus Christ. 18 No
> one has ever seen God; the only God, who is at the Father's side,
> He has made Him known.

1. The Word, verses 1–3.

    a. Why does John refer to Jesus as the Word?

b. What are the attributes of the Word in verses 1–3?

2. In addition to John 1:3, discuss how other scriptural references develop the role of God in creation. Refer to Genesis 1:1–3. How did God create the heavens and earth—and light?

a. Read Genesis 1:26. Why does God refer to making man in "Our" image? (See these other plural references: Genesis 3:22; 11:7; Isaiah 6:8. See also references to God's council: 1 Kings 22:19–23; Job 15:8; Jeremiah 23:8.)

b. What details of Christ's role in creation does Hebrews 1:1–3 add?

3. Referring again to John 1:1–3, how might Jewish and Gentile readers differ in their views of John's opening, "In the beginning was the Word"?

4. John 1:4–5, 7–9 refers to life and light in Christ. Life and light are common themes in John. John refers to life forty-seven times and to light twenty-four times. Consider the following references:

   a. What aspects of life are referred to in the following verses?

   Genesis 1:26–27

   Psalm 139:13–14

   Ephesians 2:10

b. What aspects of life are referred to in John 3:16 and John 6:51?

John 3:16

John 6:51

c. Jesus said, "The thief comes only to steal and kill and destroy. I came that they may have life and have it abundantly" (John 10:10). What does this promise of "abundant life" or "life to the full" mean to you?

5. What does John mean by describing Jesus as light, the light of men? Refer to the following verses.

   a. Jesus said, "I am the way, and the truth, and the life. No one comes to the Father except through Me" (John 14:6).

b. "I am the light of the world. Whoever follows Me will not walk in darkness, but will have the light of life" (John 8:12).

c. "The LORD is God, and He has made His light to shine upon us" (Psalm 118:27).

6. In John 1:6–8, 15, John the Baptist gives testimony that Jesus is the Son of God, Christ the Lord. What are the other testimonies that bear this truth? See John 5:31–40.

7. In John 1:10, the world does not recognize Jesus as Creator or Lord. What do those who receive the Word and those who reject the Word have in common?

    a. What "right" do those who receive the Word have?

    b. How would you summarize the essence of the Gospel message presented in these passages? Compare to John 3:16.

    c. What blocks understanding and recognition that Jesus is God Incarnate, life, and light?

8. In John 1:14–18, John introduces another name for Jesus—the "only Son"—as he discusses Jesus in the context of John the Baptist and Moses.

    a. What does Jesus have in common with the prophets?

    b. How is Jesus different from other prophets?

9. What is John's purpose in writing his Gospel account? See John 20:30–31.

Closing Prayer and Blessing

A Miraculous Birth—John

But the angel said to him, "Do not be afraid, Zechariah, for your prayer has been heard, and your wife Elizabeth will bear you a son, and you shall call his name John." (Luke 1:13)

Prayers

____

____

____

____

____

Background

Luke is the only non-Jewish New Testament writer. He does not quote the Old Testament for his Gentile audience but translates Hebrew words into their Greek equivalents. One of his emphases is that Jesus is the Savior of the world, not just the Messiah of the Jews. For example, his genealogy of Jesus goes back to Adam whereas Matthew's goes back to Abraham, the father of the Jewish nation. Luke wrote both the Book of Acts and this Gospel, but he was not one of the twelve disciples. He carefully investigated everything and wrote an orderly account so that his benefactor, Theophilus, might know with certainty that everything he was taught about Jesus was true. Luke was a companion to Paul on some of his travels. Paul refers to him as a doctor, so it is assumed he was a physician.

Read Luke 1:1–17.

> [1] Inasmuch as many have undertaken to compile a narrative of the
> things that have been accomplished among us, [2] just as those who
> from the beginning were eyewitnesses and ministers of the word
> have delivered them to us, [3] it seemed good to me also, having
> followed all things closely for some time past, to write an orderly
> account for you, most excellent Theophilus, [4] that you may have
> certainty concerning the things you have been taught.

> [5] In the days of Herod, king of Judea, there was a priest named
> Zechariah, of the division of Abijah. And he had a wife from the
> daughters of Aaron, and her name was Elizabeth. [6] And they were
> both righteous before God, walking blamelessly in all the com-
> mandments and statutes of the Lord. [7] But they had no child, be-
> cause Elizabeth was barren, and both were advanced in years.
>
> [8] Now while he was serving as priest before God when his division
> was on duty, [9] according to the custom of the priesthood, he was
> chosen by lot to enter the temple of the Lord and burn incense.
> [10] And the whole multitude of the people were praying outside
> at the hour of incense. [11] And there appeared to him an angel of
> the Lord standing on the right side of the altar of incense. [12] And
> Zechariah was troubled when he saw him, and fear fell upon him.
> [13] But the angel said to him, "Do not be afraid, Zechariah, for your
> prayer has been heard, and your wife Elizabeth will bear you a
> son, and you shall call his name John. [14] And you will have joy and
> gladness, and many will rejoice at his birth, [15] for he will be great
> before the Lord. And he must not drink wine or strong drink,
> and he will be filled with the Holy Spirit, even from his mother's
> womb. [16] And he will turn many of the children of Israel to the
> Lord their God, [17] and he will go before Him in the spirit and
> power of Elijah, to turn the hearts of the fathers to the children,
> and the disobedient to the wisdom of the just, to make ready for
> the Lord a people prepared."

Luke commonly uses rulers to place the Gospel events in a historical context. He places John's birth during the time of King Herod, who ruled from 37–4 BC. In verses 5–6, Luke says Zechariah and Elizabeth were upright and righteous and from the line of Aaron.

1. Refer to 1 Chronicles 23:13 and summarize the significance of Luke's statement.

2. Luke follows their righteousness with "but" in verse 7, and then mentions that they were childless.

    a. What was the prevailing view of being childless in this time period?

    b. Can you think of other Bible examples that demonstrate God's love

3. What might Zechariah have felt as he went to do his duty in the temple? Refer to the following verses:

    a. Read Luke 1:9; see Proverbs 16:33.

    b. Read Luke 1:10; see Psalm 141:2.

4. Gabriel told Zechariah the extraordinary news of his extraordinary son, who was never to take wine or fermented drink. This command is for someone set apart for God's special purpose (a Nazirite vow) described by Moses in Numbers 6:1–4. What promises did Gabriel make to Zechariah in the temple?

Read Luke 1:18–25.

> 18 And Zechariah said to the angel, "How shall I know this? For I
> am an old man, and my wife is advanced in years." 19 And the an-
> gel answered him, "I am Gabriel. I stand in the presence of God,
> and I was sent to speak to you and to bring you this good news.
> 20 And behold, you will be silent and unable to speak until the
> day that these things take place, because you did not believe my
> words, which will be fulfilled in their time." 21 And the people
> were waiting for Zechariah, and they were wondering at his delay
> in the temple. 22 And when he came out, he was unable to speak
> to them, and they realized that he had seen a vision in the temple.
> And he kept making signs to them and remained mute. 23 And
> when his time of service was ended, he went to his home.
>
> 24 After these days his wife Elizabeth conceived, and for five
> months she kept herself hidden, saying, 25 "Thus the Lord has
> done for me in the days when He looked on me, to take away my
> reproach among people."

5. What was Zechariah's response to the angel?

    a. What do Gabriel's words tell us about God's power and control?

b. What were the people expecting Zechariah to do when he came from the temple? See Numbers 6:22–27.

READ LUKE 1:36–45.

Gabriel is speaking to Mary:

> [36] "And behold, your relative Elizabeth in her old age has also con-
> ceived a son, and this is the sixth month with her who was called
> barren. [37] For nothing will be impossible with God." [38] And Mary
> said, "Behold, I am the servant of the Lord; let it be to me accord-
> ing to your word." And the angel departed from her.
>
> [39] In those days Mary arose and went with haste into the hill coun-
> try, to a town in Judah, [40] and she entered the house of Zechariah
> and greeted Elizabeth. [41] And when Elizabeth heard the greeting
> of Mary, the baby leaped in her womb. And Elizabeth was filled
> with the Holy Spirit, [42] and she exclaimed with a loud cry, "Blessed
> are you among women, and blessed is the fruit of your womb! [43]
> And why is this granted to me that the mother of my Lord should
> come to me? [44] For behold, when the sound of your greeting came
> to my ears, the baby in my womb leaped for joy. [45] And blessed is
> she who believed that there would be a fulfillment of what was
> spoken to her from the Lord."

6. Here we learn Elizabeth and Mary were related. Remember that Elizabeth is in "old age" and Mary is a young betrothed woman. What might this experience and three-month visit have meant to Mary and Elizabeth?

READ LUKE 1:57–66.

> 57 Now the time came for Elizabeth to give birth, and she bore a
> son. 58 And her neighbors and relatives heard that the Lord had
> shown great mercy to her, and they rejoiced with her. 59 And
> on the eighth day they came to circumcise the child. And they
> would have called him Zechariah after his father, 60 but his moth-
> er answered, "No; he shall be called John." 61 And they said to
> her, "None of your relatives is called by this name." 62 And they
> made signs to his father, inquiring what he wanted him to be
> called. 63 And he asked for a writing tablet and wrote, "His name
> is John." And they all wondered. 64 And immediately his mouth
> was opened and his tongue loosed, and he spoke, blessing God.
> 65 And fear came on all their neighbors. And all these things were
> talked about through all the hill country of Judea, 66 and all who
> heard them laid them up in their hearts, saying, "What then will
> this child be?" For the hand of the Lord was with him.

7. What miracle takes place?

8. What does it mean that the Lord's hand was with John?

READ LUKE 1:67–80—ZECHARIAH'S SONG.

> 67 And his father Zechariah was filled with the Holy Spirit and
> prophesied, saying, 68 "Blessed be the Lord God of Israel, for He
> has visited and redeemed His people 69 and has raised up a horn of
> salvation for us in the house of His servant David, 70 as He spoke
> by the mouth of His holy prophets from of old, 71 that we should
> be saved from our enemies and from the hand of all who hate us;
> 72 to show the mercy promised to our fathers and to remember

His holy covenant, [73] the oath that He swore to our father Abraham, to grant us [74] that we, being delivered from the hand of our
enemies, might serve Him without fear, [75] in holiness and righteousness before Him all our days. [76] And you, child, will be called
the prophet of the Most High; for you will go before the Lord to
prepare His ways, [77] to give knowledge of salvation to His people
in the forgiveness of their sins, [78] because of the tender mercy of
our God, whereby the sunrise shall visit us from on high [79] to give
light to those who sit in darkness and in the shadow of death, to
guide our feet into the way of peace."

[80] And the child grew and became strong in spirit, and he was in
the wilderness until the day of his public appearance to Israel.

9. Zechariah's song is called the Benedictus and is used is the Matins liturgy. Zechariah quotes promises the Lord made to Israel through the prophet Isaiah to redeem Israel and to raise up a Savior to save Israel from their enemies. How did Israel expect their salvation to happen?

10. What is the purpose of salvation? Refer to verses 74–75 in Zechariah's song.

11. Zechariah repeated the angel Gabriel's proclamation that his son would go before the Lord in the spirit and power of Elijah. Refer to the following verses and summarize how John's life would fulfill prophecy.

    a. Luke 1:16–17; see Malachi 3:1; 4:5–6.

b. Luke 3:3–6

12. God unfolded His plan of salvation to Israel from the time of Abraham to the time of Christ so that John and Jesus were born at the right time and place. How has God unfolded His plan of salvation in your life? Write a song or prayer of praise to God this week using the special events of your own spiritual pilgrimage.

Closing Prayer and Blessing

A Miraculous Birth—Jesus

"Behold, the virgin shall conceive and bear a son,
and they shall call His name Immanuel"
(which means, God with us). (Matthew 1:23)

Prayers

____

____

____

____

____

Background

Place the following events in chronological order.

____ The angel's visit to Mary telling her of Jesus' coming birth

____ The angel's visit to Zechariah about John's coming birth

____ The visit of the Magi

____ Joseph's discovery of Mary's pregnancy

____ The visit of the shepherds

____ The appearance of the star

____ The birth of Jesus

____ The birth of John

____ The existence of Christ

____ The circumcision of Jesus.

1. What difference does it make that these occurred in a chronologically identifiable order?

Read Matthew 1:18–25.

> [18] Now the birth of Jesus Christ took place in this way. When His mother Mary had been betrothed to Joseph, before they came together she was found to be with child from the Holy Spirit. [19] And her husband Joseph, being a just man and unwilling to put her to shame, resolved to divorce her quietly. [20] But as he considered these things, behold, an angel of the Lord appeared to him in a dream, saying, "Joseph, son of David, do not fear to take Mary as your wife, for that which is conceived in her is from the Holy Spirit. [21] She will bear a son, and you shall call His name Jesus, for He will save His people from their sins." [22] All this took place to fulfill what the Lord had spoken by the prophet [Isaiah 7:14]: [23] "Behold, the virgin shall conceive and bear a son, and they shall call His name Immanuel" (which means, God with us). [24] When Joseph woke from sleep, he did as the angel of the Lord commanded him: he took his wife, [25] but knew her not until she had given birth to a son. And he called His name Jesus.

2. What do we learn about Joseph's character (v. 19)?

3. Many Christians are skeptical about the virgin birth. Why is it so significant? See Isaiah 7:10–14 for the context of Matthew's quote from the prophet.

4. What did the angels reveal to Mary and Joseph about the baby to be born to them? (See Matthew 1:20–23; Luke 1:31–35.)

READ LUKE 2:1–20—JESUS' BIRTH.

> 1 In those days a decree went out from Caesar Augustus that all the world should be registered. 2 This was the first registration when Quirinius was governor of Syria. 3 And all went to be registered, each to his own town. 4 And Joseph also went up from Galilee, from the town of Nazareth, to Judea, to the city of David, which is called Bethlehem, because he was of the house and lineage of David, 5 to be registered with Mary, his betrothed, who was with child. 6 And while they were there, the time came for her to give birth. 7 And she gave birth to her firstborn son and wrapped Him in swaddling cloths and laid Him in a manger, because there was no place for them in the inn.
>
> 8 And in the same region there were shepherds out in the field, keeping watch over their flock by night. 9 And an angel of the Lord appeared to them, and the glory of the Lord shone around them, and they were filled with great fear. 10 And the angel said

> to them, "Fear not, for behold, I bring you good news of great
> joy that will be for all the people. [11] For unto you is born this day
> in the city of David a Savior, who is Christ the Lord. [12] And this
> will be a sign for you: you will find a baby wrapped in swaddling
> cloths and lying in a manger." [13] And suddenly there was with the
> angel a multitude of the heavenly host praising God and saying,
> [14] "Glory to God in the highest, and on earth peace among those
> with whom He is pleased!"
>
> [15] When the angels went away from them into heaven, the shep-
> herds said to one another, "Let us go over to Bethlehem and see
> this thing that has happened, which the Lord has made known
> to us." [16] And they went with haste and found Mary and Joseph,
> and the baby lying in a manger. [17] And when they saw it, they
> made known the saying that had been told them concerning this
> child. [18] And all who heard it wondered at what the shepherds told
> them. [19] But Mary treasured up all these things, pondering them
> in her heart. [20] And the shepherds returned, glorifying and prais-
> ing God for all they had heard and seen, as it had been told them.

5. Luke commonly makes use of historical references surrounding Jesus' birth, life, and ministry, as in Luke 2:1–2. Why would this have been important to his readers?

6. Why did Mary and Joseph go to Bethlehem? Multiple choice!

   a. God told them to go there.

   b. Caesar made them go there.

   c. They wanted to see their family roots.

   d. All of the above . . . sort of.

7. What did the innkeeper say to Joseph when he got there?

8. Why did God first announce Jesus' birth to shepherds and not to others with more influence?

9. What do we learn about Jesus' identity from the angel's announcement to the shepherds?

10. Who were the first evangelists? What was their message?

11. What was Mary's response to all that was happening?

READ MATTHEW 2:1–12—THE VISIT OF THE MAGI.

> 1 Now after Jesus was born in Bethlehem of Judea in the days of
> Herod the king, behold, wise men from the east came to Jerusa-
> lem, 2 saying, "Where is He who has been born king of the Jews?
> For we saw His star when it rose and have come to worship Him."
> 3 When Herod the king heard this, he was troubled, and all Jeru-
> salem with him; 4 and assembling all the chief priests and scribes
> of the people, he inquired of them where the Christ was to be

born. 5 They told him, "In Bethlehem of Judea, for so it is written
by the prophet: 6 'And you, O Bethlehem, in the land of Judah, are
by no means least among the rulers of Judah; for from you shall
come a ruler who will shepherd My people Israel.'"

7 Then Herod summoned the wise men secretly and ascertained
from them what time the star had appeared. 8 And he sent them
to Bethlehem, saying, "Go and search diligently for the child, and
when you have found Him, bring me word, that I too may come
and worship Him." 9 After listening to the king, they went on their
way. And behold, the star that they had seen when it rose went before them until it came to rest over the place where the child was.
10 When they saw the star, they rejoiced exceedingly with great
joy. 11 And going into the house, they saw the child with Mary His
mother, and they fell down and worshiped Him. Then, opening
their treasures, they offered Him gifts, gold and frankincense and
myrrh. 12 And being warned in a dream not to return to Herod,
they departed to their own country by another way.

12. Who were the Magi (Wise Men)?

    a. How many Magi visited Jesus?

    b. Where did they come from?

c. How might they have determined to come to Jerusalem seeking "the king of the Jews"?

13. The gifts of the Magi were both useful and symbolic. See references to their uses in Leviticus 2:1 and Song of Solomon 3:6.

    a. How were the gifts useful?

    b. How were they symbolic?

14. Why did God become a man?

15. *What is God saying to me* by sending His Son into the world through a virgin, born as a baby, laid in a manger, celebrated by angels, and worshiped by shepherds and Wise Men? What am I going to do about it?

Closing Prayer and Blessing

John the Baptist and the Baptism of Jesus

And when Jesus was baptized, immediately He went up from the water, and behold, the heavens were opened to Him, and He saw the Spirit of God descending like a dove and coming to rest on Him; and behold, a voice from heaven said, "This is My beloved Son, with whom I am well pleased."

(Matthew 3:16–17)

Prayers

____

____

____

____

____

Background

Luke's historical setting (see Luke 3:1–2) places Jesus' Baptism between AD 26 and 29, when Jesus was about thirty years old (Luke 3:23). He does this by referencing the Roman rulers of the day. The dates of their rule are a matter of historical record.

Tiberius Caesar	AD 14–37
Pontius Pilate	AD 26–36
Herod Tetrarch	4 BC–AD 39
Philip Tetrarch	4 BC–AD 34
Lysanias Tetrarch	4 BC–AD 29
Annas High Priest	AD 6–15
Caiaphas High Priest	AD 18–36 (son-in-law to Annas)

Tiberius Caesar ruled from AD 14–37 and was the third Caesar after Julius and Augustus Caesar. Augustus Caesar ordered the census at the time of Christ's birth and ruled from 27 BC to AD 14.

Pontius Pilate was prefect (military governor) of Judea from AD 26–36 during Jesus' ministry and presided over His trial and crucifixion. A building stone with his inscription was found in Caesarea in 1961. Pilate was recalled to Rome in AD 37 for his brutal handling of a civil uprising in Samaria (without establishing peace).

Herod Tetrarch was a son of Herod the Great. He reigned from 4 BC to AD 39. After his father's death in 4 BC (1 BC is also commonly cited), Judea and Galilee were divided into four segments, each ruled by a "tetrarch" (one of four rulers). Herod Tetrarch was also referred to as Herod Antipas or simply as Antipas. He is infamous for beheading John the Baptist after John criticized him for divorcing his wife to marry Herodias, his brother's wife. Antipas also took part in Jesus' trial hoping Jesus would perform a miracle after Pilate sent Jesus to him.

Philip Tetrarch was tetrarch from 4 BC to AD 34. There is little historical record of him.

Lysanias Tetrarch was tetrarch from 4 BC to AD 29. There is little historical record of him.

Two high priests are mentioned: Annas and his son-in-law, Caiaphas, who served as high priest during Jesus' ministry. Annas was high priest from AD 6–15 and Caiaphas from AD 18–36. Following Jewish custom, Annas would have served as high priest until his death (Numbers 35:25, 28; Joshua 20:6), but he was removed from service by the Romans. Caiaphas and Annas plotted together to murder Jesus. Caiaphas spoke the prophetic words that it would be better for a man (Jesus) to die for the people than for the whole nation to perish (John 11:50). Caiaphas also warned Peter and John not to speak of Jesus after they had healed a man crippled from birth in the name of Jesus (Acts 4:6, 18).

READ LUKE 3:1–20.

> [1] In the fifteenth year of the reign of Tiberius Caesar, Pontius Pi-
> late being governor of Judea, and Herod being tetrarch of Gali-
> lee, and his brother Philip tetrarch of the region of Ituraea and
> Trachonitis, and Lysanias tetrarch of Abilene, [2] during the high
> priesthood of Annas and Caiaphas, the word of God came to John
> the son of Zechariah in the wilderness. [3] And he went into all the
> region around the Jordan, proclaiming a baptism of repentance
> for the forgiveness of sins. [4] As it is written in the book of the
> words of Isaiah the prophet,

"The voice of one crying in the wilderness: 'Prepare the way of the
Lord, make His paths straight. [5] Every valley shall be filled, and
every mountain and hill shall be made low, and the crooked shall
become straight, and the rough places shall become level ways,
[6] and all flesh shall see the salvation of God.'"

[7] He said therefore to the crowds that came out to be baptized
by him, "You brood of vipers! Who warned you to flee from the
wrath to come? [8] Bear fruits in keeping with repentance. And do
not begin to say to yourselves, 'We have Abraham as our father.'
For I tell you, God is able from these stones to raise up children
for Abraham. [9] Even now the axe is laid to the root of the trees.
Every tree therefore that does not bear good fruit is cut down and
thrown into the fire."

[10] And the crowds asked him, "What then shall we do?" [11] And
he answered them, "Whoever has two tunics is to share with him
who has none, and whoever has food is to do likewise." [12] Tax col-
lectors also came to be baptized and said to him, "Teacher, what
shall we do?" [13] And he said to them, "Collect no more than you
are authorized to do." [14] Soldiers also asked him, "And we, what
shall we do?" And he said to them, "Do not extort money from
anyone by threats or by false accusation, and be content with your
wages."

[15] As the people were in expectation, and all were questioning in
their hearts concerning John, whether he might be the Christ,
[16] John answered them all, saying, "I baptize you with water, but
He who is mightier than I is coming, the strap of whose sandals I
am not worthy to untie. He will baptize you with the Holy Spirit
and fire. [17] His winnowing fork is in His hand, to clear His thresh-
ing floor and to gather the wheat into His barn, but the chaff He
will burn with unquenchable fire."

[18] So with many other exhortations he preached good news to the
people. [19] But Herod the tetrarch, who had been reproved by him
for Herodias, his brother's wife, and for all the evil things that
Herod had done, [20] added this to them all, that he locked up John
in prison.

1. Refer to Luke 3:3–6. How would you summarize John the Baptist's mission?

2. Matthew 3:4 describes John's clothing and diet. "Now John wore a garment of camel's hair and a leather belt around his waist, and his food was locusts and wild honey." See also Mark 1:6. What is the significance of the details in 2 Kings 1:8 and Malachi 4:5, and why were they important to Matthew's Gospel?

3. Crowds came to John for Baptism and repentance. Luke 3:7 tells us John addressed the crowd as a "brood of vipers," but Matthew 3:7 states that John was specifically addressing the Pharisees and Sadducees who came to see him. Judging by John's response, why do you think the Pharisees and Sadducees came to him?

4. Refer to Luke 3:8–15. What practical ways did John tell the people to produce fruit in keeping with repentance?

5. Compare Luke 3:16 (above) to John 7:38; Acts 2:38; and 1 Corinthians 12:13. How was John's Baptism different from Jesus' Baptism?

READ MATTHEW 3:13–17.

> [13] Then Jesus came from Galilee to the Jordan to John, to be bap-
> tized by him. [14] John would have prevented Him, saying, "I need
> to be baptized by You, and do You come to me?" [15] But Jesus an-
> swered him, "Let it be so now, for thus it is fitting for us to ful-
> fill all righteousness." Then he consented. [16] And when Jesus was
> baptized, immediately He went up from the water, and behold,
> the heavens were opened to Him, and He saw the Spirit of God
> descending like a dove and coming to rest on Him; [17] and behold,
> a voice from heaven said, "This is My beloved Son, with whom I
> am well pleased."

6. Jesus' Baptism is one of only three accounts of God's spoken voice in the Gospels. What is God's message here? What was the purpose of Jesus' Baptism?

7. Luther reminds us to remember our Baptism *daily* with contrition and repentance. Read the following verses and reflect on the promises we have through Baptism.

   Whoever believes and is baptized will be saved, but whoever does not believe will be condemned. (Mark 16:16)

   But when the goodness and loving kindness of God our Savior appeared, He saved us, not because of works done by us in righteousness, but according to His own mercy, by the washing of regeneration and renewal of the Holy Spirit, whom He poured out on us richly through Jesus Christ our Savior, so that being justified by His grace we might become heirs according to the hope of eternal life. The saying is trustworthy, and I want you to insist on these things, so that those who have believed in God may be careful to devote themselves to good works. These things are excellent and profitable for people. (Titus 3:4–8)

   Go therefore and make disciples of all nations, baptizing them in the name of the Father and of the Son and of the Holy Spirit, teaching them to observe all that I have commanded you. And behold, I am with you always, to the end of the age. (Matthew 28:19–20)

   a. What gifts and promises of God do we have through Baptism?

   Mark 16:16

   Titus 3:4–8

   Matthew 28:19–20

b. What confidence and comfort do we have through Baptism?

8. There are many applications to our daily lives in these Scriptures. What applications resonate the most with you?

Closing Prayer and Blessing

Jesus' Temptation in the Wilderness

And Jesus answered him, "It is written,
'You shall worship the Lord your God,
and Him only shall you serve.'" (Luke 4:8)

Prayers

Read Luke 4:1–13.

1 And Jesus, full of the Holy Spirit, returned from the Jordan
and was led by the Spirit in the wilderness 2 for forty days, being
tempted by the devil. And He ate nothing during those days. And
when they were ended, He was hungry. 3 The devil said to Him,
"If You are the Son of God, command this stone to become bread."
4 And Jesus answered him, "It is written, 'Man shall not live by
bread alone.'" 5 And the devil took Him up and showed Him all
the kingdoms of the world in a moment of time, 6 and said to
Him, "To You I will give all this authority and their glory, for it has
been delivered to me, and I give it to whom I will. 7 If You, then,
will worship me, it will all be Yours." 8 And Jesus answered him, "It
is written, 'You shall worship the Lord your God, and Him only
shall you serve.'"

9 And he took Him to Jerusalem and set Him on the pinnacle of
the temple and said to Him, "If You are the Son of God, throw
Yourself down from here, 10 for it is written, 'He will command
His angels concerning you, to guard you,' 11 and 'On their hands
they will bear you up, lest you strike your foot against a stone.'"

12 And Jesus answered him, "It is said, 'You shall not put the Lord
your God to the test.'" 13 And when the devil had ended every
temptation, he departed from Him until an opportune time.

1. In Luke 4:2, what was significant about the forty days? (See Exodus 34:28 and 1 Kings 19:7–8.)

2. In Luke 4:2–3, Satan begins by attacking Jesus' identity. There are two ways to see this attack:

    1. "If You are . . ."—to cast doubt

    2. "If [since] You are . . . then . . ."

    a. Which seems more likely in Jesus' case?

b. How have you seen either of these attacks on identity in your life or the lives of others?

3. We will use a memory device to remember Jesus' temptations—they all begin with *A*. Satan first tempts Jesus to satisfy His hunger and turn stones into bread (Luke 4:2–3). What is the basis of Satan's temptation, Appetite, Ambition, or Acclaim?

    a. God created us with certain desires. What other things do we hunger for?

    b. What can make these desires sinful?

c. How did Jesus counter Satan's first temptation? Read Deuteronomy 8:1–3 and consider the context. Of what Old Testament situation would this have reminded Jesus?

4. Refer to Luke 4:5–7. Satan's second temptation was to offer Jesus all the authority and glory of the world's kingdoms if only He would worship him. What is the core desire of this temptation, Appetite, Ambition, or Acclaim?

   a. How could Satan claim he had dominion over all the glory of the world's kingdoms? Some helpful references are John 14:30; Ephesians 6:11–12; and 2 Corinthians 4:4.

In Luke 4:8, Jesus countered Satan with the Scripture passage known as the greatest commandment from Deuteronomy 6:5, 13:

b. How would our ambitions be shaped if God's greatest command was at the center of our decisions?

c. Satan's promise of glory came with a price—"If You will worship me." We all have ambitions in life. What are some of yours and what are the potential threats that accompany your ambitions?

5. In Luke 4:9–11, Satan quotes Psalm 91:11–12 in his third temptation and challenges Jesus to throw Himself off the top of the temple so that His angels will rescue Him. To what desire does this temptation appeal, Appetite, Ambition, or Acclaim?

a. How did Satan misapply Psalm 91:9–12? Refer to Psalm 91:1–13 for context.

b. How did Jesus counter Satan in Luke 4:12?

c. How are we tempted to put God to the test?

6. Where are you most vulnerable to attacks from Satan in Appetite, Ambition, or Applause (Acclaim)?

7. What is the warning in Luke 4:13? See also 1 Peter 5:8.

8. What will help you against the attacks of Satan when you are tempted?

Closing Prayer and Blessing

JESUS AND NICODEMUS

*Jesus answered, "Truly, truly, I say to you,
unless one is born of water and the Spirit,
he cannot enter the kingdom of God." (John 3:5)*

PRAYERS

____

____

____

____

READ JOHN 3:1–15.

> [1] Now there was a man of the Pharisees named Nicodemus, a rul-
> er of the Jews. [2] This man came to Jesus by night and said to Him,
> "Rabbi, we know that You are a teacher come from God, for no
> one can do these signs that You do unless God is with him." [3]
> Jesus answered him, "Truly, truly, I say to you, unless one is born
> again he cannot see the kingdom of God." [4] Nicodemus said to
> Him, "How can a man be born when he is old? Can he enter a
> second time into his mother's womb and be born?" [5] Jesus an-
> swered, "Truly, truly, I say to you, unless one is born of water and
> the Spirit, he cannot enter the kingdom of God. [6] That which is
> born of the flesh is flesh, and that which is born of the Spirit is
> spirit. [7] Do not marvel that I said to you, 'You must be born again.'
> [8] The wind blows where it wishes, and you hear its sound, but you
> do not know where it comes from or where it goes. So it is with
> everyone who is born of the Spirit."
>
> [9] Nicodemus said to Him, "How can these things be?" [10] Jesus
> answered him, "Are you the teacher of Israel and yet you do not
> understand these things? [11] Truly, truly, I say to you, We speak of
> what We know, and bear witness to what We have seen, but you
> do not receive Our testimony. [12] If I have told you earthly things
> and you do not believe, how can you believe if I tell you heavenly
> things? [13] No one has ascended into heaven except He who de-

scended from heaven, the Son of Man. 14 And as Moses lifted up
the serpent in the wilderness, so must the Son of Man be lifted up,
15 that whoever believes in Him may have eternal life."

1. What do you learn about Nicodemus in John 3:1–2?

2. Why do you think he came at night?

3. What does his statement in verse 2 tell you about the Jewish leaders?

4. Why might Jesus have been so straightforward with him?

5. How does Jesus' interaction with him differ from His interactions with other Pharisees? See Matthew 23:13, 15.

6. To what different kinds of birth do Jesus and Nicodemus refer?

7. What was Jesus' point in comparing spiritual birth to the wind?

8. What does Jesus say in regard to Nicodemus's inability to understand?

9. At other times in its history, Israel's leaders were not equipped to lead, either through their corruption or ignorance. What was God's solution? See Ezekiel 34:1–4, 15.

10. How does Jesus' reference to the serpent in the wilderness illustrate what Jesus has come to do? See Numbers 21:4–9.

11. According to John 3:13–15, what is Jesus' claim about Himself?

READ JOHN 3:16–21.

> 16 For God so loved the world, that He gave His only Son, that
> whoever believes in Him should not perish but have eternal life.
> 17 For God did not send His Son into the world to condemn the
> world, but in order that the world might be saved through Him.
> 18 Whoever believes in Him is not condemned, but whoever does
> not believe is condemned already, because he has not believed
> in the name of the only Son of God. 19 And this is the judgment:
> the light has come into the world, and people loved the darkness
> rather than the light because their works were evil. 20 For every-
> one who does wicked things hates the light and does not come to
> the light, lest his works should be exposed. 21 But whoever does
> what is true comes to the light, so that it may be clearly seen that
> his works have been carried out in God.

12. Refer to verses 16–18 for questions a, b, and c.

    a. What do you find remarkable about God in these verses?

b. What is His desire, according to verse 17?

c. What condemns a person?

13. How would you define "born again" as used by Jesus?

14. Refer to verse 21. How will faith be revealed?

15. How do you see the development of faith in Nicodemus's life? See John 3:2; 7:50–51; 19:39.

16. What is your takeaway from today's lesson?

17. What difference will it make in your actions this week?

Closing Prayer and Blessing

The Samaritan Woman at the Well

Whoever drinks of the water that I will give him will never be thirsty again. The water that I will give him will become in him a spring of water welling up to eternal life. (John 4:14)

Prayers

____

____

____

____

Background

The animosity between the Jews and Samaritans was over seven hundred years old. The Samaritans were the remnant of the Northern Kingdom of Israel who split off from the Southern Kingdom of Judah after the death of Solomon (1 Kings 12:1–24). The Northern Kingdom was conquered and obliterated in 722 BC by Assyria (2 Kings 17:6–18). Assyria's practice was to destabilize conquered nations so the people could not revolt. The leadership of the conquered nation was murdered, and the people were scattered throughout the Assyrian empire. Other conquered peoples were brought in to settle their conquered territory. Consequently, the new people in a territory had no national or religious identity.

The Samaritans were the assimilation of survivors and displaced conquered peoples who were sent to settle Samaria. The Samaritan's religion was based on the Law of Moses—the first five books of the Old Testament. Second Kings 17:24–28 explains that after Assyria resettled the territory of Israel with conquered people, those people were afflicted by lion attacks because they did not worship the Lord. The king of Assyria ordered one of the captured priests from Israel to be sent to the people to teach them to worship the Lord. They worshiped on Mount Gerizim rather than the temple in Jerusalem. Mount Gerizim and Mount Ebal were the places where Moses commanded Joshua to read the Law to the Israelites and erect an altar after they entered the Promised Land. Mount Gerizim is a higher mountain than the Temple Mount in Jerusalem, and the Samaritans believed that it was God's chosen site for His temple (Exodus

25:8). In the time of the Persians, the Samaritans constructed their temple on Mount Gerizim, and the Jews destroyed it before Jesus' birth.

READ JOHN 4:1–30.

> [1] Now when Jesus learned that the Pharisees had heard that Jesus was making and baptizing more disciples than John [2] (although Jesus Himself did not baptize, but only His disciples), [3] He left Judea and departed again for Galilee. [4] And He had to pass through Samaria. [5] So He came to a town of Samaria called Sychar, near the field that Jacob had given to his son Joseph. [6] Jacob's well was there; so Jesus, wearied as He was from His journey, was sitting beside the well. It was about the sixth hour.
>
> [7] A woman from Samaria came to draw water. Jesus said to her, "Give Me a drink." [8] (For His disciples had gone away into the city to buy food.) [9] The Samaritan woman said to Him, "How is it that You, a Jew, ask for a drink from me, a woman of Samaria?" (For Jews have no dealings with Samaritans.) [10] Jesus answered her, "If you knew the gift of God, and who it is that is saying to you, 'Give Me a drink,' you would have asked Him, and He would have given you living water." [11] The woman said to Him, "Sir, You have nothing to draw water with, and the well is deep. Where do You get that living water? [12] Are You greater than our father Jacob? He gave us the well and drank from it himself, as did his sons and his livestock." [13] Jesus said to her, "Everyone who drinks of this water will be thirsty again, [14] but whoever drinks of the water that I will give him will never be thirsty again. The water that I will give him will become in him a spring of water welling up to eternal life." [15] The woman said to Him, "Sir, give me this water, so that I will not be thirsty or have to come here to draw water."
>
> [16] Jesus said to her, "Go, call your husband, and come here." [17] The woman answered Him, "I have no husband." Jesus said to her, "You are right in saying, 'I have no husband'; [18] for you have had five husbands, and the one you now have is not your husband. What you have said is true." [19] The woman said to Him, "Sir, I perceive that You are a prophet. [20] Our fathers worshiped on this mountain, but You say that in Jerusalem is the place where people ought to worship." [21] Jesus said to her, "Woman, believe Me, the hour is coming when neither on this mountain nor in Jerusalem will you worship the Father. [22] You worship what you do not know; we worship what we know, for salvation is from the Jews. [23] But the hour is coming, and is now here, when the true worshipers will worship the Father in spirit and truth, for the Fa-

> ther is seeking such people to worship Him. [24] God is spirit, and
> those who worship Him must worship in spirit and truth." [25] The
> woman said to Him, "I know that Messiah is coming (He who is
> called Christ). When He comes, He will tell us all things." [26] Jesus
> said to her, "I who speak to you am He."
>
> [27] Just then His disciples came back. They marveled that He was
> talking with a woman, but no one said, "What do You seek?" or,
> "Why are You talking with her?" [28] So the woman left her water
> jar and went away into town and said to the people, [29] "Come, see
> a man who told me all that I ever did. Can this be the Christ?"
> [30] They went out of the town and were coming to Him.

1. Refer to John 4:4. Why did Jesus go to Galilee through Samaria?

2. There are many suppositions about the sin of the Samaritan woman, but her sin is not the focus of the story. What can we conclude about the Samaritan woman by her reaction to Jesus from the passage?

    a. Verse 9

    b. Verse 12

c. Verses 16–18

d. Verses 19–20

e. Verse 25

f. Verse 29

3. Compare the Samaritan religion to the Jewish religion of Jesus' day.

   a. How were they similar? different?

b. Now consider Christianity today. What religions share similarities with Christianity but end up with different beliefs?

4. Reread John 4:9–10. The woman's comments could have easily started a discussion about religion or sexuality. How does Jesus respond to her comment?

5. In John 4:10, Jesus' reference to the *gift of God* is the only occurrence of the Greek word *dorea* in the Bible. The word conveys the idea of a gift that is incomprehensibly wonderful and beyond measure. In this passage, Jesus speaks of living water with the divine insight. Read the following references to highlight His meaning:

a. In Jeremiah 2:13, God uses living water to describe Himself. What are the broken cisterns that Jeremiah is referring to?

b. In Zechariah 14:8–9, what is the imagery of living water flowing to the east and west and in summer and winter?

c. The imagery of living water in Revelation 22:1–5.

6. Return to John 4:10–15. Does the woman have any idea what Jesus means by living water?

What is the living water that is a spring welling up to eternal life?

7. Reread verses 16–18. Does Jesus dwell on the woman's sin?

8. See verses 19–24. When the Samaritan woman recognized Jesus was a prophet, she asked Him why the Jews claimed the Samaritans worshiped on the wrong mountain, Mount Gerizim—the mountain Moses told the Israelites to proclaim God's blessings on—rather than on Mount Zion. This may have been her opportunity to clarify the historical separation between Samaritans and Jews or may have been an attempt to deflect the conversation away from herself. How did Jesus respond to the woman's comments?

9. See verse 25. The Samaritans lived with expectation of a Messiah and only accepted the five books of Moses as their Scripture. Do you find this surprising? Review the following examples of messianic prophecy from Moses and consider what the Samaritan view of the Messiah would be.

   > I will bless those who bless you, and him who dishonors you I will curse, and in you all the families of the earth shall be blessed. (Genesis 12:3)
   >
   > I will raise up for them a prophet like you from among their brothers. And I will put My words in His mouth, and He shall speak to them all that I command Him. (Deuteronomy 18:18)
   >
   > I see Him, but not now; I behold Him, but not near: a star shall come out of Jacob, and a scepter shall rise out of Israel; it shall crush the forehead of Moab and break down all the sons of Sheth. (Numbers 24:17)

10. In John 4:26, Jesus declares that He is the Messiah. What is the woman's response to Jesus' declaration?

11. What are the three things Jesus revealed to the Samaritan woman?

    1. Verse 14

    2. Verse 23

    3. Verse 26

12. In verses 31–38, what lessons did Jesus want His disciples to learn from their stay in Samaria?

13. What are Jesus' main teachings about the Holy Spirit to Nicodemus in John 3 and to the Samaritan woman at the well in John 4?

    1. John 3:3–8:

    2. John 3:16, 21:

    3. John 4:10–14:

14. This account is one of the greatest examples of winning souls and repentance in the Bible! What practical points does this passage make about witnessing to others with a different faith?

Closing Prayer and Blessing

Jesus Returns Home; Three Examples of Faith

Jesus said to him, "Go; your son will live." The man believed the word that Jesus spoke to him and went on his way. (John 4:50)

Prayers

____

____

____

____

Background

Jesus returned from Samaria and Jerusalem to begin His ministry in Galilee. This fulfilled the Scriptures: "In the former time He brought into contempt the land of Zebulun and the land of Naphtali, but in the latter time He has made glorious the way of the sea, the land beyond the Jordan, Galilee of the nations. The people who walked in darkness have seen a great light; those who dwelt in a land of deep darkness, on them has light shone" (Isaiah 9:1–2). Galilee was ethnically diverse and shared the same historic destruction as Samaria by the Assyrians seven hundred years earlier. The area was extensively resettled by Jews, and there were Jewish synagogues throughout the region.

1. Define the following words. How are their meanings different?

    a. Disciple—

b. Apostle—

c. Christian—

Read John 4:43–54—The Healing of the Nobleman's Son.

[43] After the two days He departed for Galilee. [44] (For Jesus Himself
had testified that a prophet has no honor in his own hometown.)
[45] So when He came to Galilee, the Galileans welcomed Him, having seen all that He had done in Jerusalem at the feast. For they
too had gone to the feast.

[46] So He came again to Cana in Galilee, where He had made the
water wine. And at Capernaum there was an official whose son
was ill. [47] When this man heard that Jesus had come from Judea to
Galilee, he went to Him and asked Him to come down and heal
his son, for he was at the point of death. [48] So Jesus said to him,
"Unless you see signs and wonders you will not believe." [49] The
official said to Him, "Sir, come down before my child dies." [50] Jesus
said to him, "Go; your son will live." The man believed the word
that Jesus spoke to him and went on his way. [51] As he was going
down, his servants met him and told him that his son was recov-
ering. [52] So he asked them the hour when he began to get better,
and they said to him, "Yesterday at the seventh hour the fever left
him." [53] The father knew that was the hour when Jesus had said
to him, "Your son will live." And he himself believed, and all his
household. [54] This was now the second sign that Jesus did when
He had come from Judea to Galilee.

2. Reread verses 46–47.

    The faith of the nobleman was the subject of a sermon on faith by Martin Luther in 1523. The nobleman's faith seems to be based on miracles Jesus publicly performed in Jerusalem during Passover (John 2:23; 4:45). His son was near death; we can assume all other medical means had been exhausted. Some speculation is required to interpret the depth of the nobleman's faith at the beginning of Jesus' ministry. What are some possible interpretations of the man's faith?

3. In verse 48, Jesus refers to the man wanting to see a sign, something the Pharisees would demand of Jesus throughout His ministry. At first reading, it seems oddly inappropriate here. How might Jesus' admonition against demanding signs have addressed the faith of this man, as well as the crowd of people?

4. In verses 49–50, the nobleman redirected Jesus to his son. Jesus told him that his son would live and dismissed the nobleman to return to Capernaum, about twenty-five miles away (nine to ten hours away on foot). What might the nobleman have thought about along the way?

5. Verses 51–53 say that the son was healed at the moment Jesus told the man his son would be healed. The nobleman and his household believed. How might this faith be different from the faith he started out with in Cana—particularly in light of Jesus' statement regarding a demand for a sign?

READ LUKE 4:14–30.

> [14] And Jesus returned in the power of the Spirit to Galilee, and a report about Him went out through all the surrounding country. [15] And He taught in their synagogues, being glorified by all.
>
> [16] And He came to Nazareth, where He had been brought up. And as was His custom, He went to the synagogue on the Sabbath day, and He stood up to read. [17] And the scroll of the prophet Isaiah was given to Him. He unrolled the scroll and found the place where it was written,
>
> [18] "The Spirit of the Lord is upon Me, because He has anointed Me to proclaim good news to the poor. He has sent Me to proclaim liberty to the captives and recovering of sight to the blind, to set at liberty those who are oppressed, [19] to proclaim the year of the Lord's favor."
>
> [20] And He rolled up the scroll and gave it back to the attendant and sat down. And the eyes of all in the synagogue were fixed on Him. [21] And He began to say to them, "Today this Scripture has been fulfilled in your hearing." [22] And all spoke well of Him and marveled at the gracious words that were coming from His mouth. And they said, "Is not this Joseph's son?" [23] And He said to them, "Doubtless you will quote to Me this proverb, '"Physician, heal yourself." What we have heard You did at Capernaum, do here in Your hometown as well.'" [24] And He said, "Truly, I say to you, no prophet is acceptable in his hometown. [25] But in truth, I tell you, there were many widows in Israel in the days of Elijah, when the heavens were shut up three years and six months, and a great famine came over all the land, [26] and Elijah was sent to none of them but only to Zarephath, in the land of Sidon, to a woman who was a widow. [27] And there were many lepers in Israel in the

> time of the prophet Elisha, and none of them was cleansed, but only Naaman the Syrian." [28] When they heard these things, all in the synagogue were filled with wrath. [29] And they rose up and drove Him out of the town and brought Him to the brow of the hill on which their town was built, so that they could throw Him down the cliff. [30] But passing through their midst, He went away.

6. Why did the people in Nazareth change their hearts from praise to murder?

READ LUKE 5:1–11.

The account of Jesus teaching by the lake in Luke 5 and calling Peter, James, and John follows an earlier meeting of His disciples by the Jordan after His Baptism found in John 1:35–51. The disciples who had been present at that time were Andrew, his brother Peter whom Andrew told that he had found the Christ, and Philip, who told Nathanael about finding the Messiah. These men were all from Galilee and returned there with Jesus, where He worked His miracle of turning water to wine.

> [1] On one occasion, while the crowd was pressing in on Him to hear the word of God, He was standing by the lake of Gennesaret, [2] and He saw two boats by the lake, but the fishermen had gone out of them and were washing their nets. [3] Getting into one of the boats, which was Simon's, He asked him to put out a little from the land. And He sat down and taught the people from the boat. [4] And when He had finished speaking, He said to Simon, "Put out into the deep and let down your nets for a catch." [5] And Simon answered, "Master, we toiled all night and took nothing! But at Your word I will let down the nets." [6] And when they had done this, they enclosed a large number of fish, and their nets were breaking. [7] They signaled to their partners in the other boat to come and help them. And they came and filled both the boats, so that they began to sink. [8] But when Simon Peter saw it, he fell down at Jesus' knees, saying, "Depart from me, for I am a sinful man, O Lord." [9] For he and all who were with him were astonished at the catch of fish that they had taken, [10] and so also were James and John, sons of Zebedee, who were partners with Simon. And Jesus said to Simon, "Do not be afraid; from now on you will be

> catching men." [11] And when they had brought their boats to land, they left everything and followed Him.

7. What was Jesus' purpose for the miraculous catch of fish?

8. Consider verses 4–6. Peter had worked hard all night but needed to learn a valuable lesson about his labor—a lesson we also need to learn. How would you summarize this lesson? (See also Proverbs 16:9: "The heart of man plans his way, but the LORD establishes his steps.")

9. Peter modeled a disciple's response (fill in the blank):

    a. When Peter began his encounter with Jesus on the lake, his faith was______.

    b. Peter responded to Jesus' word (or call) to _________ Him.

    c. God did a mighty work, and Peter's faith was ______________.

    d. Jesus was working to shape Peter into a different man who would _________________ His Church.

10. In verse 9, Peter and his companions were astonished when they recognized the miraculous catch was God's work and not their own. Have you ever been astonished by God's work?

Jesus found a spectrum of responses when He returned to Galilee after His Baptism and trials in the wilderness. In the nobleman, He found a desperate man who placed his hope in Jesus. The people of Nazareth praised Jesus as a man of wisdom but were ready to murder Him when He claimed to be the Messiah. In the last example, Jesus found disciples whose hearts were ready to follow Him and leave everything behind. Even with this extraordinary faith, their faith would also grow.

As we study Jesus' ministry, we will see examples of extraordinary faith and other examples of faith that is struggling like another man who pleaded for his son—"I believe; help my unbelief!" (Mark 9:24). Our faith, knowledge of Christ, and spiritual gifts grow as we exercise them. Faith grows when it is grounded in the Word and is presented with adversity, trial, and temptation. Jesus frequently admonished the disciples for their weak faith. They also needed to exercise their faith so it would become stronger to withstand future temptations and persecutions. Unlike faith, our salvation does not grow; it is complete from the moment it is received.

Closing Prayer and Blessing

Teaching in Galilee

Blessed are the poor in spirit, for theirs
is the kingdom of heaven.
(Matthew 5:3)

Prayer

____

____

____

____

Background

In Matthew 4:23–25, Jesus has been traveling throughout Galilee, teaching, preaching, and healing. Having heard about His miracles, people came from Galilee, Judea, Syria, the Decapolis, and from across the Jordan to see and hear for themselves.

The Sermon on the Mount is the first of five great discourses in Matthew. These discourses are (1) the Sermon on the Mount, (2) the sending of the twelve disciples, (3) the sermon by the lake, (4) teaching the disciples on the road, and (5) teaching in the temple courts. In the Sermon on the Mount, Jesus offers comfort to the meek and broken and then contrasts Jewish ethical and legalistic traditions with God's standards summarized in Matthew 5:48, "You therefore must be perfect, as your heavenly Father is perfect."

Read Matthew 4:23–5:12.

> [23] And He went throughout all Galilee, teaching in their synagogues and proclaiming the gospel of the kingdom and healing every disease and every affliction among the people. [24] So His fame spread throughout all Syria, and they brought Him all the sick, those afflicted with various diseases and pains, those oppressed by demons, those having seizures, and paralytics, and He healed them. [25] And great crowds followed Him from Galilee and the Decapolis, and from Jerusalem and Judea, and from beyond the Jordan.

[5:1] Seeing the crowds, He went up on the mountain, and when He
sat down, His disciples came to Him. [2] And He opened His mouth
and taught them, saying:

[3] "Blessed are the poor in spirit, for theirs is the kingdom of heaven.

[4] "Blessed are those who mourn, for they shall be comforted.

[5] "Blessed are the meek, for they shall inherit the earth.

[6] "Blessed are those who hunger and thirst for righteousness, for
they shall be satisfied.

[7] "Blessed are the merciful, for they shall receive mercy.

[8] "Blessed are the pure in heart, for they shall see God.

[9] "Blessed are the peacemakers, for they shall be called sons of
God.

[10] "Blessed are those who are persecuted for righteousness' sake,
for theirs is the kingdom of heaven.

[11] "Blessed are you when others revile you and persecute you and
utter all kinds of evil against you falsely on My account. [12] Rejoice
and be glad, for your reward is great in heaven, for so they persecuted the prophets who were before you."

1. What connection do you see between 4:23–25 and 5:3–4?

2. What does it mean to be blessed, and how is this different from "happiness"?

3. In this context, how would you define:

    a. Poor in spirit—

    b. Those who mourn—

    c. The meek—

    d. The pure in heart—

    e. Persecuted for righteousness' sake—

f. Also see the character qualities in Psalm 37:4–11.

4. What would you say is the key to being "blessed"?

5. How do the "blessed" qualities that describe people of God's kingdom relate to the promises that follow them?

6. How do these promised blessings compare with what most people of the world prize?

7. Would kingdom people be admired in our society?

READ MATTHEW 5:13–16.

> 13 You are the salt of the earth, but if salt has lost its taste, how shall
> its saltiness be restored? It is no longer good for anything except
> to be thrown out and trampled under people's feet.
>
> 14 You are the light of the world. A city set on a hill cannot be hid-
> den. 15 Nor do people light a lamp and put it under a basket, but
> on a stand, and it gives light to all in the house. 16 In the same way,
> let your light shine before others, so that they may see your good
> works and give glory to your Father who is in heaven.

8. What are some characteristics of salt and light, and how do they apply to our life as Christians?

READ MATTHEW 5:17–48.

> 17 Do not think that I have come to abolish the Law or the Proph-
> ets; I have not come to abolish them but to fulfill them. 18 For tru-
> ly, I say to you, until heaven and earth pass away, not an iota, not
> a dot, will pass from the Law until all is accomplished. 19 There-
> fore whoever relaxes one of the least of these commandments and
> teaches others to do the same will be called least in the kingdom
> of heaven, but whoever does them and teaches them will be called
> great in the kingdom of heaven. 20 For I tell you, unless your righ-
> teousness exceeds that of the scribes and Pharisees, you will never
> enter the kingdom of heaven.
>
> 21 You have heard that it was said to those of old, "You shall not

murder; and whoever murders will be liable to judgment." [22] But I say to you that everyone who is angry with his brother will be liable to judgment; whoever insults his brother will be liable to the council; and whoever says, "You fool!" will be liable to the hell of fire. [23] So if you are offering your gift at the altar and there remember that your brother has something against you, [24] leave your gift there before the altar and go. First be reconciled to your brother, and then come and offer your gift. [25] Come to terms quickly with your accuser while you are going with him to court, lest your accuser hand you over to the judge, and the judge to the guard, and you be put in prison. [26] Truly, I say to you, you will never get out until you have paid the last penny.

[27] You have heard that it was said, "You shall not commit adultery." [28] But I say to you that everyone who looks at a woman with lustful intent has already committed adultery with her in his heart. [29] If your right eye causes you to sin, tear it out and throw it away. For it is better that you lose one of your members than that your whole body be thrown into hell. [30] And if your right hand causes you to sin, cut it off and throw it away. For it is better that you lose one of your members than that your whole body go into hell.

[31] It was also said, "Whoever divorces his wife, let him give her a certificate of divorce." [32] But I say to you that everyone who divorces his wife, except on the ground of sexual immorality, makes her commit adultery, and whoever marries a divorced woman commits adultery.

[33] Again you have heard that it was said to those of old, "You shall not swear falsely, but shall perform to the Lord what you have sworn." [34] But I say to you, Do not take an oath at all, either by heaven, for it is the throne of God, [35] or by the earth, for it is His footstool, or by Jerusalem, for it is the city of the great King. [36] And do not take an oath by your head, for you cannot make one hair white or black. [37] Let what you say be simply "Yes" or "No"; anything more than this comes from evil.

[38] You have heard that it was said, "An eye for an eye and a tooth for a tooth." [39] But I say to you, Do not resist the one who is evil. But if anyone slaps you on the right cheek, turn to him the other also. [40] And if anyone would sue you and take your tunic, let him have your cloak as well. [41] And if anyone forces you to go one mile, go with him two miles. [42] Give to the one who begs from you, and do not refuse the one who would borrow from you.

[43] You have heard that it was said, "You shall love your neighbor

> and hate your enemy." 44 But I say to you, Love your enemies and
> pray for those who persecute you, 45 so that you may be sons of
> your Father who is in heaven. For He makes His sun rise on the
> evil and on the good, and sends rain on the just and on the unjust.
> 46 For if you love those who love you, what reward do you have?
> Do not even the tax collectors do the same? 47 And if you greet
> only your brothers, what more are you doing than others? Do not
> even the Gentiles do the same? 48 You therefore must be perfect,
> as your heavenly Father is perfect.

9. Jesus was concerned about the original purpose of the Law; the Pharisees were concerned about carrying out the letter of the Law. What did they miss?

10. How can our righteousness surpass that of the Pharisees?

11. Look back at Matthew 5:48. Why do you think Jesus said this?

Closing Prayer and Blessing

Jesus' Healing Ministry

And when the Lord saw her, He had compassion on her and said to her, "Do not weep." (Luke 7:13)

Prayer

____

____

____

____

Background

Jesus' preaching and miracles served four purposes: (1) they fulfilled Scripture's prophecy (Isaiah 35:5–6; 61:1–2); (2) they demonstrated that He was the Messiah, (3) they brought people to faith in Him; and (4) they demonstrated God's outpouring of compassion and love for His people. There was no set pattern or formula in Jesus' healing ministry. He frequently healed with a touch, a word, or an object. Sometimes a person had faith in Jesus, sometimes not. The only common factors were Jesus' power over sickness and death and that His Father's will was done.

Jesus' healing miracles are reminders of the restoration He brings to His fallen creatures. Just as a lame person could walk, the blind could see, and the deaf hear, at Jesus' return all the ailments that afflict our bodies will be instantly healed, and we will live before Him in perfect health in our resurrected bodies.

Read Mark 1:40–45—The Man with Leprosy.

> 40 And a leper came to Him, imploring Him, and kneeling said to
> Him, "If You will, You can make me clean." 41 Moved with pity, He
> stretched out His hand and touched him and said to him, "I will;
> be clean." 42 And immediately the leprosy left him, and he was
> made clean. 43 And Jesus sternly charged him and sent him away
> at once, 44 and said to him, "See that you say nothing to anyone,
> but go, show yourself to the priest and offer for your cleansing
> what Moses commanded, for a proof to them." 45 But he went out

> and began to talk freely about it, and to spread the news, so that Jesus could no longer openly enter a town, but was out in desolate places, and people were coming to Him from every quarter.

1. Note that this account is also in Luke 5:12–16 and Matthew 8:2–4. What did the law require of people with leprosy (Leviticus 13:45–46)?

2. Fill in the blank: The man with leprosy was healed because of his ________ and Jesus' ______________________ and ________________.

3. What was the purpose of sending the man to the priest after the healing? The law for cleansing leprosy is found in Leviticus 14 (see verses 1–9 especially).

4. The man seems to have skipped over Jesus' command (a strong warning) to make a sacrifice at the temple. Do you think God was angry with him?

5. Jesus frequently told people not to tell others but rarely said why. What was the result of the man's testimony?

READ LUKE 7:1–9; MATTHEW 8:11–13—THE FAITH OF THE CENTURION.

> [1] After He had finished all His sayings in the hearing of the peo-
> ple, He entered Capernaum. [2] Now a centurion had a servant who
> was sick and at the point of death, who was highly valued by him.
> [3] When the centurion heard about Jesus, he sent to Him elders of
> the Jews, asking Him to come and heal his servant. [4] And when
> they came to Jesus, they pleaded with Him earnestly, saying, "He
> is worthy to have You do this for him, [5] for he loves our nation,
> and he is the one who built us our synagogue." [6] And Jesus went
> with them. When He was not far from the house, the centurion
> sent friends, saying to Him, "Lord, do not trouble Yourself, for I
> am not worthy to have You come under my roof. [7] Therefore I did
> not presume to come to You. But say the word, and let my servant
> be healed. [8] For I too am a man set under authority, with soldiers
> under me: and I say to one, 'Go,' and he goes; and to another,
> 'Come,' and he comes; and to my servant, 'Do this,' and he does it."
> [9] When Jesus heard these things, He marveled at him, and turning
> to the crowd that followed Him, said, "I tell you, not even in Israel
> have I found such faith." . . .
>
> [Matthew 8:11] "I tell you, many will come from east and west and re-
> cline at table with Abraham, Isaac, and Jacob in the kingdom of
> heaven, [12] while the sons of the kingdom will be thrown into the
> outer darkness. In that place there will be weeping and gnashing
> of teeth." [13] And to the centurion Jesus said, "Go; let it be done for
> you as you have believed." And the servant was healed at that very
> moment.

Centurions were professional Roman soldiers who commanded a hundred men. Sometimes they were politically appointed, but more frequently they were promoted from the field and recognized for their leadership, bravery, and skill. Highest ranking centurions were given charge of front lines in battle and were highly paid. They were also promoted or elected to positions in civil government.

6. Why would this man send Jewish elders, who were normally antagonistic toward Jesus?

7. I am amazed that Jesus could be amazed by the centurion's faith. What does this statement imply to you?

8. Matthew includes verses 11–12 in his account in chapter 8. These verses seem a bit out of context, but what do they mean and why are they important in his Gospel?

9. The centurion's faith in Jesus' authority was held up as an example to Israel and to us. What attributes of the centurion are admirable?

READ LUKE 7:11–17—JESUS RAISES A WIDOW'S SON.

> [11] Soon afterward He went to a town called Nain, and His disciples
> and a great crowd went with Him. [12] As He drew near to the gate
> of the town, behold, a man who had died was being carried out,
> the only son of his mother, and she was a widow, and a considerable crowd from the town was with her. [13] And when the Lord saw
> her, He had compassion on her and said to her, "Do not weep."
> [14] Then He came up and touched the bier, and the bearers stood
> still. And He said, "Young man, I say to you, arise." [15] And the
> dead man sat up and began to speak, and Jesus gave him to his
> mother. [16] Fear seized them all, and they glorified God, saying,
> "A great prophet has arisen among us!" and "God has visited His
> people!" [17] And this report about Him spread through the whole
> of Judea and all the surrounding country.

This miracle shows Jesus' compassion for the broken and needy as well as His authority over death (and life). The raising of the widow's son is one of three accounts of Jesus raising the dead to life. Power over death was the ultimate sign of the Lord's reign prophesied in Isaiah 26:19 and foreshadowed Jesus' own resurrection as proof that He was the Messiah and sovereign Lord of whom the prophets spoke.

The impact of a loved one's death can be physically, mentally, and spiritually devastating. Life for widows and orphans was hard in ancient times and is hard today.

10. What are the elements of the tragedy in this account? See also Deuteronomy 24:19–22 and 26:12–13 regarding the care for widows and orphans.

11. In the context of these three healings and your own experience, discuss the role of faith in healing.

12. As you go home, consider these takeaway points from the lesson:

    1. God's grace and mercy are present in all healing.
    2. Our faith in healing is in God, in His power and compassion.
    3. We submit to God's will and timing.
    4. God's grace is not dependent on our faith.
    5. There is a spiritual danger when we think healing is dependent on our faith or another's faith.

Closing Prayer and Blessing

The Calling of Matthew

Follow Me. (Mark 2:14)

Prayers

____

____

____

____

Background

Matthew's calling takes place in Capernaum, the town Jesus lived in after He was rejected in His hometown of Nazareth. Capernaum was the site of many of Jesus' miracles. People came to Capernaum from all over Galilee and Judea to have Jesus heal their sick and to hear Him preach. Matthew, Mark, and Luke include the account of the healing of a paralytic man who was brought to Jesus through the roof of a house because so many people had gathered in the house and outside the door. When Jesus saw their faith, He healed the paralytic and forgave his sins. The Pharisees correctly discerned that only God could forgive sins but missed Christ's identity as God Incarnate. Matthew was the town's tax collector and would have witnessed the miraculous power of Jesus' word and touch.

In this lesson, we will reflect on our own calling. Does Jesus expect us as His followers to emulate the lives of the apostles and leave everything to follow Him? Or does He call us to serve Him where we are now?

Read Mark 2:13–17.

> [13] He went out again beside the sea, and all the crowd was coming
> to Him, and He was teaching them. [14] And as He passed by, He
> saw Levi the son of Alphaeus sitting at the tax booth, and He said
> to him, "Follow Me." And he rose and followed Him.
>
> [15] And as He reclined at table in his house, many tax collectors
> and sinners were reclining with Jesus and His disciples, for there
> were many who followed Him. [16] And the scribes of the Pharisees,

> when they saw that He was eating with sinners and tax collectors, said to His disciples, "Why does He eat with tax collectors and sinners?" [17] And when Jesus heard it, He said to them, "Those who are well have no need of a physician, but those who are sick. I came not to call the righteous, but sinners."

1. What are Matthew's various names?

2. Compare how people viewed Matthew to how Jesus viewed him.

3. Do you recall a time when someone's appearance surprised you once you got to know them?

4. How did Matthew respond to Jesus' call?

5. How is our calling similar to Matthew's? Summarize the following in your own words:

    a. John 15:16–17

    b. 1 Corinthians 1:2

    c. Ephesians 1:4–6

6. What has Jesus called us to?

    a. John 3:5

    b. 1 Corinthians 1:9

c. 1 John 3:1

d. 1 Peter 1:14–16

7. Jesus called His disciples to a great purpose—to minister to others and to establish His Church. Likewise, we are called to great purpose. Summarize the following verses:

    a. 1 Peter 2:9

    b. Ephesians 2:10

    c. 2 Corinthians 5:17–20

8. Jesus' apostles left their professions and livelihood to follow Him. When a rich young ruler came and asked Jesus what he must do to inherit eternal life, the Lord asked him if he had kept the moral laws. The youth said yes; he had since he was a boy. Jesus told him, "One thing you still lack. Sell all that you have and distribute to the poor, and you will have treasure in heaven; and come, follow Me" (Luke 18:22). Do you think we are commanded to do the same? What do the following verses say about your calling from

Christ? Consider Paul's example to the Thessalonians and the Colossians to help address this question. Refer to 2 Thessalonians 3:7–12 and Colossians 3:23–24.

9. What happens to God's kingdom if we don't answer God's call because we are just uncomfortable talking about Jesus to others?

10. As you go home, consider these takeaway points from the lesson:

    1. Jesus loves sinners.
    2. Jesus has foreknowledge of a person's potential.
    3. A disciple shares his love for Jesus with others.
    4. We are called to a great purpose and held securely in Christ by God's plan and grace.

Closing Prayer and Blessing

Parables concerning the Kingdom of Heaven

Other seeds fell on good soil and produced grain, some a hundredfold, some sixty, some thirty. He who has ears, let him hear. (Matthew 13:8–9)

Prayers

____

____

____

____

Background

Jesus taught about the kingdom of heaven through parables as He traveled through Galilee, Judea, and Jerusalem. The Gospel writers organized them in different ways to illustrate various themes in Jesus' teaching. Matthew organized Jesus' teaching into five great compilations:

1. **The Sermon on the Mount**—contrast of life under the letter of the Law versus the spirit of the Law. (Matthew 5–7).
2. **The Sending of the Apostles**—instructions for ministry (Matthew 10)
3. **The Sermon on the Lake**—parables on the kingdom of heaven (Matthew 13)
4. **Teachings in Capernaum**—parables on the kingdom of heaven (Matthew 18–20).
5. **Teaching in the Temple**—concerning the end of the age (Matthew 24–25).

In this lesson, we will look at Jesus' parables on the growth of God's kingdom that are included in the sermon on the lake in Matthew 13. Mark and Luke include several other parables in similar compilations. These include the following:

- The parable of the sower (Matthew, Mark, Luke)
- The lamp on a stand (Mark, Luke)
- The parable of the growing seed (Mark)
- The parable of the weeds (Matthew)
- The parable of the mustard seed and yeast (Matthew, Mark, Luke)
- The parable of the hidden treasure and the pearl (Matthew)
- The parable of the net (Matthew)

1. *Parable* is a Greek term for making a comparison or bringing side by side. Consequently, the goal of Jesus' teaching was to illustrate a spiritual truth through common, everyday experiences in the lives of His hearers. Refer to the following Scripture passages to determine the purpose that parables served in Jesus' teaching:

   a. Hosea 12:10

   b. Psalm 78:2, 4

   c. Isaiah 6:9–10

Read Matthew 13:1–23—The Parable of the Sower.

[1] That same day Jesus went out of the house and sat beside the sea. [2] And great crowds gathered about Him, so that He got into a boat and sat down. And the whole crowd stood on the beach. [3] And He told them many things in parables, saying: "A sower went out to sow. [4] And as he sowed, some seeds fell along the path, and the birds came and devoured them. [5] Other seeds fell on rocky ground, where they did not have much soil, and immediately they sprang up, since they had no depth of soil, [6] but when the sun rose they were scorched. And since they had no root, they withered away. [7] Other seeds fell among thorns, and the thorns grew up and choked them. [8] Other seeds fell on good soil and produced grain, some a hundredfold, some sixty, some thirty. [9] He who has ears, let him hear."

[10] Then the disciples came and said to Him, "Why do You speak to them in parables?" [11] And He answered them, "To you it has been given to know the secrets of the kingdom of heaven, but to them it has not been given. [12] For to the one who has, more will be given, and he will have an abundance, but from the one who has not, even what he has will be taken away. [13] This is why I speak to them in parables, because seeing they do not see, and hearing they do not hear, nor do they understand. [14] Indeed, in their case the prophecy of Isaiah is fulfilled that says: "'You will indeed hear but never understand, and you will indeed see but never perceive." [15] For this people's heart has grown dull, and with their ears they can barely hear, and their eyes they have closed, lest they should see with their eyes and hear with their ears and understand with their heart and turn, and I would heal them.'

[16] "But blessed are your eyes, for they see, and your ears, for they hear. [17] For truly, I say to you, many prophets and righteous people longed to see what you see, and did not see it, and to hear what you hear, and did not hear it.

[18] "Hear then the parable of the sower: [19] When anyone hears the word of the kingdom and does not understand it, the evil one comes and snatches away what has been sown in his heart. This is what was sown along the path. [20] As for what was sown on rocky ground, this is the one who hears the word and immediately receives it with joy, [21] yet he has no root in himself, but endures for a while, and when tribulation or persecution arises on account of the word, immediately he falls away. [22] As for what was sown among thorns, this is the one who hears the word, but the cares

of the world and the deceitfulness of riches choke the word, and
it proves unfruitful. 23 As for what was sown on good soil, this is
the one who hears the word and understands it. He indeed bears
fruit and yields, in one case a hundredfold, in another sixty, and
in another thirty."

2. What is the application of each soil where the seed (the Word) was sown?

   a. The path

   b. The rocky ground

   c. The thorns

   d. Good soil

3. What do you think of when you hear the phrases "kingdom of God" or "kingdom of heaven"?

READ MARK 4:21–25—THE PARABLE OF THE LAMP.

> 21 And He said to them, "Is a lamp brought in to be put under a
> basket, or under a bed, and not on a stand? 22 For nothing is hid-
> den except to be made manifest; nor is anything secret except to
> come to light. 23 If anyone has ears to hear, let him hear." 24 And He
> said to them, "Pay attention to what you hear: with the measure
> you use, it will be measured to you, and still more will be added to
> you. 25 For to the one who has, more will be given, and from the
> one who has not, even what he has will be taken away."

4. We normally think of the lamp as a visible demonstration of our faith through our actions and words to our neighbors. Consider reading the lamp as God's Word. What additional insights does this parable provide?

    a. Verse 21

    b. Verse 22

    c. Verses 24–25

READ MARK 4:26–29—THE PARABLE OF THE GROWING SEED.

> 26 And He said, "The kingdom of God is as if a man should scatter
> seed on the ground. 27 He sleeps and rises night and day, and the
> seed sprouts and grows; he knows not how. 28 The earth produces
> by itself, first the blade, then the ear, then the full grain in the ear.
> 29 But when the grain is ripe, at once he puts in the sickle, because
> the harvest has come."

5. How is growing seed like the kingdom of heaven?

6. How do you interpret the harvest?

READ MATTHEW 13:24–30, 36–43—THE PARABLE OF WEEDS.

> 24 He put another parable before them, saying, "The kingdom of
> heaven may be compared to a man who sowed good seed in his
> field, 25 but while his men were sleeping, his enemy came and
> sowed weeds among the wheat and went away. 26 So when the
> plants came up and bore grain, then the weeds appeared also. 27
> And the servants of the master of the house came and said to him,
> 'Master, did you not sow good seed in your field? How then does
> it have weeds?' 28 He said to them, 'An enemy has done this.' So
> the servants said to him, 'Then do you want us to go and gather
> them?' 29 But he said, 'No, lest in gathering the weeds you root up
> the wheat along with them. 30 Let both grow together until the
> harvest, and at harvest time I will tell the reapers, "Gather the
> weeds first and bind them in bundles to be burned, but gather the
> wheat into my barn."'" . . .
>
> 36 Then He left the crowds and went into the house. And His disci-
> ples came to Him, saying, "Explain to us the parable of the weeds
> of the field." 37 He answered, "The one who sows the good seed
> is the Son of Man. 38 The field is the world, and the good seed is
> the sons of the kingdom. The weeds are the sons of the evil one,
> 39 and the enemy who sowed them is the devil. The harvest is the
> end of the age, and the reapers are angels. 40 Just as the weeds are
> gathered and burned with fire, so will it be at the end of the age. 41
> The Son of Man will send His angels, and they will gather out of
> His kingdom all causes of sin and all law-breakers, 42 and throw
> them into the fiery furnace. In that place there will be weeping

> and gnashing of teeth. [43] Then the righteous will shine like the sun
> in the kingdom of their Father. He who has ears, let him hear."

7. What simple truths does this parable teach about the existence of good and evil in the world?

8. Based on the parable of the growing seed, how is God active when the weeds are growing?

READ MATTHEW 13:31–35—THE PARABLES OF THE MUSTARD SEED AND YEAST.

> [31] He put another parable before them, saying, "The kingdom of
> heaven is like a grain of mustard seed that a man took and sowed
> in his field. [32] It is the smallest of all seeds, but when it has grown it
> is larger than all the garden plants and becomes a tree, so that the
> birds of the air come and make nests in its branches."
>
> [33] He told them another parable. "The kingdom of heaven is like
> leaven that a woman took and hid in three measures of flour, till
> it was all leavened."
>
> [34] All these things Jesus said to the crowds in parables; indeed, He
> said nothing to them without a parable. [35] This was to fulfill what
> was spoken by the prophet:
>
> "I will open My mouth in parables; I will utter what has been hidden since the foundation of the world."

9. How are both the mustard seed and yeast like the kingdom of heaven?

10. Who are the birds in the parable?

11. What do the birds find in the garden that we find in the kingdom of heaven?

READ MATTHEW 13:44–50—THE PARABLES OF THE TREASURE, THE PEARL, AND THE NET.

> 44 The kingdom of heaven is like treasure hidden in a field, which a man found and covered up. Then in his joy he goes and sells all that he has and buys that field.
>
> 45 Again, the kingdom of heaven is like a merchant in search of
> fine pearls, 46 who, on finding one pearl of great value, went and
> sold all that he had and bought it.
>
> 47 Again, the kingdom of heaven is like a net that was thrown into
> the sea and gathered fish of every kind. 48 When it was full, men
> drew it ashore and sat down and sorted the good into containers but threw away the bad. 49 So it will be at the end of the age.
> The angels will come out and separate the evil from the righteous
> 50 and throw them into the fiery furnace. In that place there will be
> weeping and gnashing of teeth.

12. What is Jesus asking the crowd to do in the parable of the treasure and the pearl?

13. The parables of the treasure, pearl, and net teach us truths about our response to God's kingdom and the end of times on earth. They can also be read from a different perspective to teach us about God's love for us when we place Him (or Jesus) as the main character who is in search of us. How do the parables change when you read them this way?

14. What might our lives look like if we deeply embraced the parables of the treasure and the pearl?

Closing Prayer and Blessing

The Feeding of the Five Thousand and Jesus Walks on Water

When He went ashore He saw a great crowd, and He had compassion on them, because they were like sheep without a shepherd. And He began to teach them many things. (Mark 6:34)

Prayers

____

____

____

____

Background

The feeding of the five thousand is Jesus' only miracle cited by all four Gospel writers. It occurs after the beheading of John the Baptist as Jesus withdraws to a solitary place (Bethsaida) with His disciples to mourn John's death. The apostle John writes that it was near the time of the Passover (John 6:4), when crowds would have been gathering for a trek to Jerusalem. This is the second reference to Passover in John's Gospel, indicating one year has passed in Jesus' ministry. However, many scholars interpret the unnamed feast in John 5:1 as a Passover, which would make this the beginning of the third year of Jesus' ministry. In either interpretation, Jesus is at the height of His popularity, but the death of John the Baptist foreshadows that Calvary's approach is unstoppable and drawing near.

The location of Bethsaida is disputed. The most common locality cited is now a ruin about two miles from the coast of the Sea of Galilee and three and a half to four miles from Capernaum. It was the hometown of Peter, Andrew, and Philip.

As we read the miracle of the feeding of the five thousand, consider that it is a fulfillment of Scripture—Jesus is the Good Shepherd of Ezekiel 34:11–12, 14–16. Jesus has compassion for His people, He knows their needs, and He is sufficient to meet them.

> For thus says the Lord GOD: Behold I, I Myself will search for My sheep and will seek them out. As a shepherd seeks out his flock when he is among his sheep that have been scattered, so will I seek out My sheep. . . . I will feed them with good pasture, and on the mountain heights of Israel shall be their grazing land. There they shall lie down in good grazing land, and on rich pasture they shall feed on the mountains of Israel. I Myself will be the shepherd of My sheep, and I Myself will make them lie down, declares the Lord GOD. I will seek the lost, and I will bring back the strayed, and I will bind up the injured, and I will strengthen the weak.

READ LUKE 9:10; MARK 6:31–36; JOHN 6:5–15—JESUS FEEDS THE FIVE THOUSAND.

> Luke 9:10 On their return the apostles told Him [Jesus] all that they had done. And He took them and withdrew apart to a town called Bethsaida. . . .
>
> Mark 6:31 And He said to them, "Come away by yourselves to a desolate place and rest a while." For many were coming and going,
> and they had no leisure even to eat. 32 And they went away in the
> boat to a desolate place by themselves. 33 Now many saw them
> going and recognized them, and they ran there on foot from all
> the towns and got there ahead of them. 34 When He went ashore
> He saw a great crowd, and He had compassion on them, because they were like sheep without a shepherd. And He began to teach
> them many things. 35 And when it grew late, His disciples came to
> Him and said, "This is a desolate place, and the hour is now late.
> 36 Send them away to go into the surrounding countryside and villages and buy themselves something to eat." . . .
>
> John 6:5 Lifting up His eyes, then, and seeing that a large crowd was coming toward Him, Jesus said to Philip, "Where are we to buy
> bread, so that these people may eat?" 6 He said this to test him,
> for He Himself knew what He would do. 7 Philip answered Him,
> "Two hundred denarii worth of bread would not be enough for
> each of them to get a little." 8 One of His disciples, Andrew, Simon
> Peter's brother, said to Him, 9 "There is a boy here who has five
> barley loaves and two fish, but what are they for so many?" 10 Jesus
> said, "Have the people sit down." Now there was much grass in
> the place. So the men sat down, about five thousand in number. 11
> Jesus then took the loaves, and when He had given thanks, He distributed them to those who were seated. So also the fish, as much
> as they wanted. 12 And when they had eaten their fill, He told His
> disciples, "Gather up the leftover fragments, that nothing may be

> lost." [13] So they gathered them up and filled twelve baskets with
> fragments from the five barley loaves left by those who had eaten.
> [14] When the people saw the sign that He had done, they said, "This
> is indeed the Prophet who is to come into the world!"
>
> [15] Perceiving then that they were about to come and take Him by
> force to make Him king, Jesus withdrew again to the mountain
> by Himself.

1. There were two significant events prior to the feeding of the five thousand. John the Baptist was beheaded by King Herod, and the disciples returned from their first mission trip without Jesus. The disciples had just experienced preaching repentance, casting out demons, and healing in Jesus' name. What was Jesus seeking in His travel to Bethsaida with His disciples?

2. What did they find instead of a solitary place?

3. See Mark 6:33. How did the people get there before Jesus and His disciples arrived by boat?

4. Reread Mark 6:34–37. Compare Jesus' response to the crowd's hunger with that of the disciples.

5. Jesus specifically questioned Philip about where to buy bread for the people to eat. Jesus asked this question because Philip was from Bethsaida, and if anyone should know where to buy food it should have been Philip (or Andrew and Peter, who were also from Bethsaida). Philip said the right thing—that it was impossible. Why then did Jesus tell them, "You give them something to eat" (Mark 6:37)?

6. How had Jesus tested their faith before?

7. This is the only miracle recorded by all four Gospel writers. How was this miracle different from the others the disciples witnessed?

8. What was Jesus teaching His disciples in this test?

9. If Jesus were testing you, how would you complete His statement, "You give them something to____ ____________________"?

10. What examples did Jesus set with respect to the meal?

11. In John 6:14–15, what was the crowd's response to the miracle? What were their motives (John 6:26)?

READ MATTHEW 14:22–33—JESUS WALKS ON WATER, ANOTHER TEST.

> 22 Immediately He made the disciples get into the boat and go be-
> fore Him to the other side, while He dismissed the crowds. 23 And
> after He had dismissed the crowds, He went up on the moun-
> tain by Himself to pray. When evening came, He was there alone,
> 24 but the boat by this time was a long way from the land, beaten
> by the waves, for the wind was against them. 25 And in the fourth
> watch of the night [between 3 a.m. and 6 a.m.] He came to them,
> walking on the sea. 26 But when the disciples saw Him walking on
> the sea, they were terrified, and said, "It is a ghost!" and they cried
> out in fear. 27 But immediately Jesus spoke to them, saying, "Take
> heart; it is I. Do not be afraid."
>
> 28 And Peter answered Him, "Lord, if it is You, command me to
> come to You on the water." 29 He said, "Come." So Peter got out of
> the boat and walked on the water and came to Jesus. 30 But when
> he saw the wind, he was afraid, and beginning to sink he cried
> out, "Lord, save me." 31 Jesus immediately reached out His hand
> and took hold of him, saying to him, "O you of little faith, why did
> you doubt?" 32 And when they got into the boat, the wind ceased.
> 33 And those in the boat worshiped Him, saying, "Truly You are
> the Son of God."

NOTE: Mark 6:52 says the disciples' hearts were hardened after Jesus stepped into the boat. Their hearts were not hardened in opposition to Jesus and His ministry, but they were hardened in spiritual understanding. They failed to grasp the purpose and full meaning of the miracle of bread and fish as well as the stilling of the storm.

12. Compare this encounter with a storm to the disciples' previous test by a storm. See Matthew 8:23–27.

13. What does Matthew 14:28 reveal about Peter's faith since the previous test?

14. In view of these miracles, what events are you encountering that seem too great to take to Jesus in prayer?

Closing Prayer and Blessing

Jesus, the Bread of Life

Jesus said to them, "I am the bread of life;
whoever comes to Me shall not hunger,
and whoever believes in Me shall never thirst." (John 6:35)

Prayers

____

____

____

____

Background

The account of Jesus declaring that He was the bread of life sent down from heaven immediately followed His miraculous feeding of a crowd of five thousand men plus women and children. After giving thanks to God for the two fish and five loaves of bread, Jesus multiplied the gift of the food and fed the crowd with twelve baskets full of leftovers. Afterward, Jesus and the disciples returned to Capernaum to find the crowd waiting and searching for Him. This was the same crowd who witnessed His miraculous healings in Capernaum and Bethsaida, who heard Him preach, and who were among the five thousand miraculously fed on the hills of Israel the day before. They wanted to make Jesus their king to provide for their every need.

Read John 6:22–40.

> 22 On the next day the crowd that remained on the other side of
> the sea saw that there had been only one boat there, and that Jesus
> had not entered the boat with His disciples, but that His disciples
> had gone away alone. 23 Other boats from Tiberias came near the
> place where they had eaten the bread after the Lord had given
> thanks. 24 So when the crowd saw that Jesus was not there, nor His
> disciples, they themselves got into the boats and went to Caper-
> naum, seeking Jesus.
>
> 25 When they found Him on the other side of the sea, they said to
> Him, "Rabbi, when did You come here?" 26 Jesus answered them,

"Truly, truly, I say to you, you are seeking Me, not because you saw signs, but because you ate your fill of the loaves. 27 Do not work for the food that perishes, but for the food that endures to eternal life, which the Son of Man will give to you. For on Him God the Father has set His seal." 28 Then they said to Him, "What must we do, to be doing the works of God?" 29 Jesus answered them, "This is the work of God, that you believe in Him whom He has sent." 30 So they said to Him, "Then what sign do You do, that we may see and believe You? What work do You perform? 31 Our fathers ate the manna in the wilderness; as it is written, 'He gave them bread from heaven to eat.'" 32 Jesus then said to them, "Truly, truly, I say to you, it was not Moses who gave you the bread from heaven, but My Father gives you the true bread from heaven. 33 For the bread of God is He who comes down from heaven and gives life to the world." 34 They said to Him, "Sir, give us this bread always."

35 Jesus said to them, "I am the bread of life; whoever comes to Me shall not hunger, and whoever believes in Me shall never thirst. 36 But I said to you that you have seen Me and yet do not believe. 37 All that the Father gives Me will come to Me, and whoever comes to Me I will never cast out. 38 For I have come down from heaven, not to do My own will but the will of Him who sent Me. 39 And this is the will of Him who sent Me, that I should lose nothing of all that He has given Me, but raise it up on the last day. 40 For this is the will of My Father, that everyone who looks on the Son and believes in Him should have eternal life, and I will raise him up on the last day."

1. See verses 25–27. Why was the crowd looking for Jesus?

2. Jesus admonishes the crowd for chasing after food. What does He tell them they should pursue?

3. Reread verse 29. What work does God require for eternal life?

4. In verse 30, what does the crowd's demand for a miraculous sign reveal about an unbelieving heart?

5. See verses 31–34. What miracle would the crowd like to see Jesus perform—continually?

6. How is Jesus like the manna the crowd was asking for?

7. What do the following verses teach about our eternal security? (Fill in the blank.)

   a. Verse 37: All those the Father gives ______________________________
   ____.

   b. Verse 37: Jesus will never ____________________________________.

   c. Verse 38: Jesus does the _________________________ of the Father.

   d. Verse 39: The will of the Father is that ______________ shall be lost, but ___________________ raised on the Last Day.

   e. Verse 40: The will of the Father is that everyone who _____________ ____ will have eternal life.

READ JOHN 6:41–59.

> [41] So the Jews grumbled about Him, because He said, "I am the bread that came down from heaven." [42] They said, "Is not this Jesus, the son of Joseph, whose father and mother we know? How does He now say, 'I have come down from heaven'?" [43] Jesus answered them, "Do not grumble among yourselves. [44] No one can come to Me unless the Father who sent Me draws him. And I will raise him up on the last day. [45] It is written in the Prophets, 'And they will all be taught by God.' Everyone who has heard and learned from the Father comes to Me— [46] not that anyone has seen the Father except He who is from God; He has seen the Father. [47] Truly, truly, I say to you, whoever believes has eternal life. [48] I am the bread of life. [49] Your fathers ate the manna in the wilderness, and they died. [50] This is the bread that comes down from heaven, so that one may eat of it and not die. [51] I am the living bread that came down from heaven. If anyone eats of this bread, he will live forever. And the bread that I will give for the life of the world is My flesh."
>
> [52] The Jews then disputed among themselves, saying, "How can this man give us His flesh to eat?" [53] So Jesus said to them, "Truly, truly, I say to you, unless you eat the flesh of the Son of Man and drink His blood, you have no life in you. [54] Whoever feeds on My flesh and drinks My blood has eternal life, and I will raise him up on the last day. [55] For My flesh is true food, and My blood is true drink. [56] Whoever feeds on My flesh and drinks My blood abides in Me, and I in him. [57] As the living Father sent Me, and I live because of the Father, so whoever feeds on Me, he also will live because of Me. [58] This is the bread that came down from heaven, not like the bread the fathers ate, and died. Whoever feeds on this bread will live forever." [59] Jesus said these things in the synagogue, as He taught at Capernaum.

8. See verses 41–42. The crowd knows Jesus can work miracles and teach with authority. What can't they accept? How is this similar to today?

9. In round 2 of the conversation, Jesus pointedly repeats His claims with greater emphasis and uses prophetic language—similar to parables. Fill in the blanks:

    a. Verse 44: No one can believe in Jesus unless the Father ______________.

    b. Verses 45–46: Jesus has seen God because He was ________________________.

    c. Verse 47: Whoever believes Jesus is sent by God from heaven has ______________ __________.

10. In verses 48–58, Jesus repeats His teaching about being manna and bread from heaven, except this time His language becomes prophetic—very similar to teaching in parables. Do you recall the purposes of this type of teaching?

    a. Psalm 78:2, 4

    b. Hosea 12:9–10

    c. Isaiah 6:9–10

11. The meaning of John 6:48–58 is difficult to unravel even considering the purposes for prophetic language. What are some of the benefits of eating the flesh of the Son of Man and drinking His blood?

    a. Verses 50, 53, 58

    b. Verse 56

    c. Discuss what it means to you to “eat the flesh of the Son of Man and drink His blood” (John 6:53).

READ JOHN 6:60–71.

> 60 When many of His disciples heard it, they said, "This is a hard
> saying; who can listen to it?" 61 But Jesus, knowing in Himself that
> His disciples were grumbling about this, said to them, "Do you
> take offense at this? 62 Then what if you were to see the Son of Man
> ascending to where He was before? 63 It is the Spirit who gives life;
> the flesh is no help at all. The words that I have spoken to you are
> spirit and life. 64 But there are some of you who do not believe."
> (For Jesus knew from the beginning who those were who did not
> believe, and who it was who would betray Him.) 65 And He said,
> "This is why I told you that no one can come to Me unless it is
> granted him by the Father."
>
> 66 After this many of His disciples turned back and no longer
> walked with Him. 67 So Jesus said to the twelve, "Do you want to
> go away as well?" 68 Simon Peter answered Him, "Lord, to whom
> shall we go? You have the words of eternal life, 69 and we have
> believed, and have come to know, that You are the Holy One of
> God." 70 Jesus answered them, "Did I not choose you, the twelve?
> And yet one of you is a devil." 71 He spoke of Judas the son of Si-
> mon Iscariot, for he, one of the twelve, was going to betray Him.

12. Clearly no one understood Jesus' teaching. How did He explain Himself to the disciples in verse 63?

13. Controversy about the meaning of John 6:48–58 continues today. Some denominations emphasize aspects of verse 55, others emphasize verse 63.

    a. Some Christians believe Communion is a sacrament, while others believe it is an ordinance. Luther's Small Catechism teaches that the word *sacrament* is from the Greek meaning "mystery." The mystery is how God does His work through the Sacraments of Baptism and Communion. The two Sacraments share common features:

1. They are a sacred act.

2. They are instituted by God (Christ).

3. God joins His Word and Himself to a visible element (water, wine, bread).

4. Through these means, God offers, gives, and seals the forgiveness of sins earned by Christ.

b. Some Christians believe the sacraments are ordinances, a prescribed practice that is symbolic of God's promises and have the following features in common:

1. They are ordered by Christ.

2. They were practiced by the Early Church.

3. They are symbols, not required for salvation but practiced to remember Christ's sacrifice for the forgiveness of our sin.

4. The union with God in these ordinances is spiritual.

14. How do these two interpretations (sacrament or ordinance) impact Communion practices in the following denominations? Match the denomination with the beliefs listed below.

A. Catholic B. Lutheran C. Methodist
D. Baptist E. Quaker

1. Bread and wine (grape juice) are symbols provided by God for spiritual communion with Christ to express our thanks for His sacrifice.

2. Elements remain as bread and wine, but the body and blood of Christ are in miraculous and mysterious union with the elements for the forgiveness of sin.

3. Every action in life is consecrated to God as an act of worship; sacraments are not practiced.

4. Elements are miraculously changed to the body and blood of Christ when consecrated by the priest (or pastor) for the forgiveness of sin.

5. The Lord's Table is open to all adults and children, baptized and unbaptized, to commune with the presence of Christ through bread and grape juice (as a substitute for wine).

Closing Prayer and Blessing

Jesus, the Good Shepherd

I am the good shepherd. The good shepherd lays down His life for the sheep. (John 10:11)

Prayers

____

____

____

____

Background

John 10 is a continuation of the conflict between Jesus and the Pharisees in Jerusalem. The conflict began in chapter 2 with the cleansing of the temple and continued with increasing intensity when Jesus visited Jerusalem for each of the three annual festivals. John 10:1–21 immediately follows the account of the healing of the man born blind and is a discussion between Jesus and the Pharisees who excommunicated the healed man and were planning to murder Jesus. The second part of the passage, verses 22–42, occurs in Jerusalem months later but includes the same themes. Chapters 2, 3, 5, and 7–10 could be woven together to form one account. Jesus again mixes His language between the spiritual allegory and the prophetic.

Read Numbers 27:16–17; John 10:1–21.

> Numbers 27:16 Let the Lord, the God of the spirits of all flesh, appoint
> a man over the congregation [17] who shall go out before them and
> come in before them, who shall lead them out and bring them in,
> that the congregation of the Lord may not be as sheep that have
> no shepherd. . . .
>
> John 10:1 "Truly, truly, I say to you, he who does not enter the sheep-
> fold by the door but climbs in by another way, that man is a thief
> and a robber. [2] But he who enters by the door is the shepherd
> of the sheep. [3] To him the gatekeeper opens. The sheep hear his
> voice, and he calls his own sheep by name and leads them out.
> [4] When he has brought out all his own, he goes before them, and

the sheep follow him, for they know his voice. 5 A stranger they
will not follow, but they will flee from him, for they do not know
the voice of strangers." 6 This figure of speech Jesus used with
them, but they did not understand what He was saying to them.

7 So Jesus again said to them, "Truly, truly, I say to you, I am the
door of the sheep. 8 All who came before Me are thieves and robbers, but the sheep did not listen to them. 9 I am the door. If anyone enters by Me, he will be saved and will go in and out and
find pasture. 10 The thief comes only to steal and kill and destroy.
I came that they may have life and have it abundantly. 11 I am
the good shepherd. The good shepherd lays down His life for the
sheep. 12 He who is a hired hand and not a shepherd, who does
not own the sheep, sees the wolf coming and leaves the sheep and
flees, and the wolf snatches them and scatters them. 13 He flees
because he is a hired hand and cares nothing for the sheep. 14 I am
the good shepherd. I know My own and My own know Me, 15 just
as the Father knows Me and I know the Father; and I lay down
My life for the sheep. 16 And I have other sheep that are not of this
fold. I must bring them also, and they will listen to My voice. So
there will be one flock, one shepherd. 17 For this reason the Father
loves Me, because I lay down My life that I may take it up again.
18 No one takes it from Me, but I lay it down of My own accord.
I have authority to lay it down, and I have authority to take it up
again. This charge I have received from My Father."

19 There was again a division among the Jews because of these
words. 20 Many of them said, "He has a demon, and is insane; why
listen to Him?" 21 Others said, "These are not the words of one
who is oppressed by a demon. Can a demon open the eyes of the
blind?"

1. In this passage, Jesus uses a figure of speech to reveal additional aspects of His character as Messiah. John tells us the people who were listening did not understand the word picture. As you read through the story, describe what each image represents and list a few of the characteristics of each.

    a. The sheepfold or sheep pen

b. The gatekeeper

c. The shepherd

d. The gate or door

e. Thieves and robbers

f. Hired hand

g. The sheep

h. Other sheep

i. My Father

2. Life in the pen under the gatekeeper may be safe and secure, but it was not the life the Good Shepherd meant for His sheep. He called the sheep out of the pen and led them out to good pasture. Likewise, Jesus came to give us life, an abundant life or life to the full (v. 10). What does His promise of abundant life mean to you?

3. In verses 11–15, what do you learn about Jesus' care and relationship with you?

4. In verse 16, what does Jesus reveal about His flock?

5. Why does Jesus stress that the Good Shepherd lays His life down for His sheep?

6. Compare Ezekiel 34:11–16 and John 10:11–18. Identify parallels between these two readings.

   Ezekiel 34:11 For thus says the Lord God: Behold, I, I Myself will search
   for My sheep and will seek them out. 12 As a shepherd seeks out
   his flock when he is among his sheep that have been scattered, so
   will I seek out My sheep, and I will rescue them from all places
   where they have been scattered on a day of clouds and thick darkness. 13 And I will bring them out from the peoples and gather
   them from the countries, and will bring them into their own land.
   And I will feed them on the mountains of Israel, by the ravines,
   and in all the inhabited places of the country. 14 I will feed them
   with good pasture, and on the mountain heights of Israel shall be
   their grazing land. There they shall lie down in good grazing land,
   and on rich pasture they shall feed on the mountains of Israel. 15 I
   Myself will be the shepherd of My sheep, and I Myself will make
   them lie down, declares the Lord God. 16 I will seek the lost, and

> I will bring back the strayed, and I will bind up the injured, and I will strengthen the weak, and the fat and the strong I will destroy. I will feed them in justice.

a. Ezekiel 34:11

b. Ezekiel 34:13

c. Ezekiel 34:14

7. Name some things your Good Shepherd has done for you.

Closing Prayer and Blessing

The Lord's Prayer

Pray then like this: "Our Father in heaven, hallowed be Your name." (Matthew 6:9)

Prayers

____

____

____

____

Background

The remaining lessons in the Gospel study occur during Jesus' Judean ministry. Matthew, Mark, and Luke organize the accounts of Jesus' teachings and miracles into two large groups: accounts that occur in Galilee and accounts that occur in Judea. Although there are chronological similarities between the authors, they are not necessarily strict chronologies but may represent compilations of teachings that occurred while Jesus was in either location traveling to and from Jerusalem. John describes Jesus' practice of going to Jerusalem from Galilee for three annual pilgrimage festivals that included Passover. Some general observations on Jesus' Judean ministry are the following:

1. Matthew and Mark include only a few chapters on Jesus' Judean ministry.
2. John 10:22, 40 points out that Jesus went to Jerusalem for the Feast of Dedication in the winter (December) and remained in the area around Judea until the Passover of His crucifixion (March/April).
3. Luke includes ten chapters on the Judean ministry beginning with Jesus setting out for Jerusalem in 9:51 and ending with the triumphant entry in 19:28. The ten chapters are a compilation of teachings, not a chronology, as is evident by Jesus' several departures for Jerusalem.

    a. Luke 9:51: Jesus resolutely sets out for Jerusalem.

    b. 10:38: Jesus ministers in Bethany (two to three miles from Jerusalem).

    c. 13:22: Jesus makes His way to Jerusalem.

d. 13:31–34: Jesus laments over Jerusalem.

e. 17:11: Jesus goes on His way to Jerusalem.

f. 18:31: Jesus tells His disciples that they are going to Jerusalem.

g. 18:35–19:9: Jesus heals and preaches in Jericho.

h. 19:28: Jesus enters Jerusalem on Palm Sunday.

4. Luke includes six major themes in his extended compilation of teaching in Judea. It is in this compilation that we find the Lord's teaching on prayer.

    a. Prayer

    b. Conflict with the Pharisees

    c. Healing on the Sabbath

    d. Judgment and end of days

    e. Kingdom of God taught in parables

    f. Discipleship

READ MATTHEW 6:7–15 AND LUKE 11:1–4.

1. Can you think of any reason the accounts of the Lord's Prayer are different in Luke and Matthew?

MATTHEW 6:7–15	LUKE 11:1–4
[7] "And when you pray, do not heap up empty phrases as the Gentiles do, for they think that they will be heard for their many words. [8] Do not be like them, for your father knows what you need before you ask Him. [9] Pray then like this:	[1] Now Jesus was praying in a certain place, and when He finished, one of His disciples said to Him, "Lord, teach us to pray, as John taught his disciples." [2] And He said to them, "When you pray, say:
"Our Father in heaven, hallowed be Your name.	"Father, hallowed be Your name.
[10] Your kingdom come,	Your kingdom come.

MATTHEW 6:7–15 CONT.	LUKE 11:1–4 CONT.
Your will be done, on earth as it is in heaven.	
[11] Give us this day our daily bread,	[3] Give us each day our daily bread,
[12] and forgive us our debts,	[4] and forgive us our sins,
as we also have forgiven our debtors.	for we ourselves forgive everyone who is indebted to us.
[13] And lead us not into temptation,	And lead us not into temptation."
but deliver us from evil.	
[14] For if you forgive others their trespasses, your heavenly Father will also forgive you, [15] but if you do not forgive others their trespasses, neither will your Father forgive your trespasses."	

2. Read Matthew 6:5–8 to consider the context of Jesus' teaching on prayer. What types of prayers are not pleasing to God?

3. Martin Luther referred to the Lord's Prayer as "the most martyred prayer on earth." What was he getting at?

4. Look up the Lord's Prayer in Luther's Small Catechism. Luther viewed the structure of the Lord's Prayer as an introduction, seven petitions, and a

conclusion. He encouraged Christians to think about what each petition meant. What do they mean to you? Read each petition and write your response.

a. Introduction—Our Father who art in heaven.

See Romans 8:15–16.

b. First Petition—Hallowed be Thy name.

See Exodus 20:7, the Second Commandment.

c. Second Petition—Thy kingdom come.

Refer to John 3:5; Romans 14:17.

d. Third Petition—Thy will be done on earth as it is in heaven.

e. Fourth Petition—Give us this day our daily bread.

Also refer to Matthew 6:25, 33; Philippians 4:19.

f. Fifth Petition—And forgive us our trespasses as we forgive those who trespass against us.

g. Sixth Petition—And lead us not into temptation.

Refer to the following verses:

Let no one say when he is tempted, "I am being tempted by God," for God cannot be tempted with evil, and He Himself tempts no one. (James 1:13)

Simon, Simon, behold, Satan demanded to have you, that he might sift you like wheat, but I have prayed for you that your faith may not fail. And when you have turned again, strengthen your brothers. (Luke 22:31–32)

h. Seventh Petition—But deliver us from evil.

Refer to 1 Peter 5:8–9; Ephesians 6:12–13.

i. Conclusion—For Thine is the kingdom and the power and the glory forever and ever. Amen.

READ LUKE 11:5–13.

5 And He said to them, "Which of you who has a friend will go
to him at midnight and say to him, 'Friend, lend me three loaves,
6 for a friend of mine has arrived on a journey, and I have nothing to set before him'; 7 and he will answer from within, 'Do not
bother me; the door is now shut, and my children are with me in
bed. I cannot get up and give you anything'? 8 I tell you, though he
will not get up and give him anything because he is his friend, yet
because of his impudence he will rise and give him whatever he
needs. 9 And I tell you, ask, and it will be given to you; seek, and

you will find; knock, and it will be opened to you. [10] For everyone who asks receives, and the one who seeks finds, and to the one who knocks it will be opened. [11] What father among you, if his son asks for a fish, will instead of a fish give him a serpent; [12] or if he asks for an egg, will give him a scorpion? [13] If you then, who are evil, know how to give good gifts to your children, how much more will the heavenly Father give the Holy Spirit to those who ask Him!"

5. What encouragement do the following verses give us?

   a. Verses 5–8

   b. Verses 9–10

   c. Verses 11–13

Read Luke 18:1–8.

[1] And He told them a parable to the effect that they ought always to pray and not lose heart. [2] He said, "In a certain city there was a judge who neither feared God nor respected man. [3] And there was a widow in that city who kept coming to him and saying, 'Give me justice against my adversary.' [4] For a while he refused,

> but afterward he said to himself, 'Though I neither fear God nor respect man, [5] yet because this widow keeps bothering me, I will give her justice, so that she will not beat me down by her continual coming.'" [6] And the Lord said, "Hear what the unrighteous judge says. [7] And will not God give justice to His elect, who cry to Him day and night? Will He delay long over them? [8] I tell you, He will give justice to them speedily. Nevertheless, when the Son of Man comes, will He find faith on earth?"

6. What is Jesus teaching us about prayer through the parable of the persistent widow?

7. Describe a time you felt like the persistent widow in prayer.

READ LUKE 18:9–17.

> [9] He also told this parable to some who trusted in themselves that they were righteous, and treated others with contempt: [10] "Two men went up into the temple to pray, one a Pharisee and the other a tax collector. [11] The Pharisee, standing by himself, prayed thus: 'God, I thank You that I am not like other men, extortioners, unjust, adulterers, or even like this tax collector. [12] I fast twice a week; I give tithes of all that I get.' [13] But the tax collector, standing far off, would not even lift up his eyes to heaven, but beat his breast, saying, 'God, be merciful to me, a sinner!' [14] I tell you, this man went down to his house justified, rather than the other. For everyone who exalts himself will be humbled, but the one who humbles himself will be exalted."
>
> [15] Now they were bringing even infants to Him that He might

touch them. And when the disciples saw it, they rebuked them.
16 But Jesus called them to Him, saying, "Let the children come to
Me, and do not hinder them, for to such belongs the kingdom of
God. 17 Truly, I say to you, whoever does not receive the kingdom
of God like a child shall not enter it."

8. What sin is Jesus condemning with the parable of the Pharisee and the tax collector?

9. Why is true faith humble?

Closing Prayer and Blessing

Jesus, Tell Us Plainly, Are You the Christ?!

"If You are the Christ, tell us plainly." Jesus answered them,
"I told you, and you do not believe."
(John 10:24–25)

Prayers

____

____

____

____

Background

John records the greatest question of all time asked of Jesus: "If You are the Christ, tell us plainly" (John 10:24). Jesus' response was plain and understood by all. He did tell them, but they did not believe. In a previous confrontation (John 5), Jesus pointed to those who testified for Him, including John the Baptist; Jesus' own miracles; His work of preaching, teaching, and healing; Moses in the Book of Deuteronomy; and God His Father. The greatest proof would be His resurrection. "Who is Jesus?" remains the most profound and life-changing question to be answered by every person.

John 10:22–42 describes a debate at the Feast of Dedication, or Hanukkah. Hanukkah was a Jewish holiday that celebrated the purification of the temple by Judas Maccabaeus in December of 165 BC. Solomon's colonnade was believed to be part of the original temple.

Read John 10:22–42.

> [22] At that time the Feast of Dedication took place at Jerusalem. It
> was winter, [23] and Jesus was walking in the temple, in the colon-
> nade of Solomon. [24] So the Jews gathered around Him and said
> to Him, "How long will You keep us in suspense? If You are the
> Christ, tell us plainly." [25] Jesus answered them, "I told you, and
> you do not believe. The works that I do in My Father's name bear

> witness about Me, 26 but you do not believe because you are not among My sheep. 27 My sheep hear My voice, and I know them, and they follow Me. 28 I give them eternal life, and they will never perish, and no one will snatch them out of My hand. 29 My Father, who has given them to Me, is greater than all, and no one is able to snatch them out of the Father's hand. 30 I and the Father are one."
>
> 31 The Jews picked up stones again to stone Him. 32 Jesus answered them, "I have shown you many good works from the Father; for which of them are you going to stone Me?" 33 The Jews answered Him, "It is not for a good work that we are going to stone You but for blasphemy, because You, being a man, make Yourself God." 34 Jesus answered them, "Is it not written in your Law, 'I said, you are gods'? 35 If He called them gods to whom the word of God came—and Scripture cannot be broken— 36 do you say of Him whom the Father consecrated and sent into the world, 'You are blaspheming,' because I said, 'I am the Son of God'? 37 If I am not doing the works of My Father, then do not believe Me; 38 but if I do them, even though you do not believe Me, believe the works, that you may know and understand that the Father is in Me and I am in the Father." 39 Again they sought to arrest Him, but He escaped from their hands.
>
> 40 He went away again across the Jordan to the place where John had been baptizing at first, and there He remained. 41 And many came to Him. And they said, "John did no sign, but everything that John said about this man was true." 42 And many believed in Him there.

1. In verses 22–25, why do the Jews ask Jesus if He is the Christ? (Refer to John 8:58–59, the last time Jesus plainly told the Pharisees He was the Christ.)

2. What promises does Jesus make in verses 25–30? Why is each precious to you?

3. See verse 33. The punishment for blasphemy was death by stoning (Leviticus 24:16). What did Jesus' enemies understand about the law and not believe about Jesus? What were they trying to do?

4. See verses 34–38. Jesus quoted Psalm 82:6 in response to the Pharisees' confrontation with Him. This must have frustrated and confounded them to see the reference in Scripture that men are referred to as "gods" because God created them and calls them His "sons." The passage from verse 34 to verse 38 is a bit difficult to follow, so how would you summarize Jesus' claim that He is God's Son?

5. Reread verses 40–42. After His conflicts with the Jews, Jesus withdrew from Jerusalem to the wilderness, where He continued His ministry to the people. Other times, He simply withdrew to pray during the stress of His ministry. How do you remain spiritually focused during times of stress?

6. Review the previous conflict with the Jews in Jerusalem recorded in John 5:30–47. What are the testimonies Jesus points to as proof that He is the Messiah?

7. What are some of the highlights in this chapter that teach you about your relationship with Christ?

Jesus did not fit the idea held by many earnest, God-fearing Jews of whom the Messiah would be. Would the Messiah be God's mighty warrior or God's Suffering Servant (Isaiah 52; 53)? In God's perfect plan and timing, the answer is both; all Scripture must be fulfilled. Following are a few examples of common views held by the Jews and the Gospel message about Jesus.

Jewish Perspective	Jesus' Revelation
The Messiah will save Israel.	The name *Jesus* means "Yahweh saves." Jesus was born to save His people from their sins (Matthew 1:21).
The Messiah will establish a kingdom in Israel that will be the center of all world government, both for Jews and Gentiles (Isaiah 2:2–4; 11:10; 42:1).	The kingdom Jesus spoke of was spiritual—no one could enter it unless they were born again by water and Spirit (John 3:3–5).
The Messiah will reestablish Jewish religious law as the law of the land (Jeremiah 33:15). Jesus disrespected the Law by healing on the Sabbath.	Jesus came to fulfill the Law (Matthew 5:17) and establish a new covenant through His blood sacrifice (Matthew 26:28; Luke 22:20). Jesus healed on the Sabbath to demonstrate that love and compassion for others was a perfect fulfillment of the Law.
The Messiah will return all exiles to their homeland (Isaiah 11:11–12).	Jesus drew all people to Himself when He was lifted up to be crucified (John 12:32). "For God so loved the world, that He gave His only Son, that whoever believes in Him should not perish but have eternal life" (John 3:16).

8. How do these comparisons impact your views toward your Jewish friends and acquaintances?

Closing Prayer and Blessing

Miracle in Bethany

Jesus said to her, "I am the resurrection and the life.
Whoever believes in Me, though he die,
yet shall he live." (John 11:25)

Prayer

Background

The opposition to Jesus in Jerusalem is growing. Jesus has withdrawn across the Jordan to the place where John baptized (John 10:39–40). But despite the opposition, many people continue to see Him.

Read John 11:1–16.

> [1] Now a certain man was ill, Lazarus of Bethany, the village of
> Mary and her sister Martha. [2] It was Mary who anointed the Lord
> with ointment and wiped His feet with her hair, whose brother
> Lazarus was ill. [3] So the sisters sent to Him, saying, "Lord, he
> whom You love is ill." [4] But when Jesus heard it He said, "This
> illness does not lead to death. It is for the glory of God, so that the
> Son of God may be glorified through it."
>
> [5] Now Jesus loved Martha and her sister and Lazarus. [6] So, when
> He heard that Lazarus was ill, He stayed two days longer in the
> place where He was. [7] Then after this He said to the disciples,
> "Let us go to Judea again." [8] The disciples said to Him, "Rabbi, the
> Jews were just now seeking to stone You, and are You going there
> again?" [9] Jesus answered, "Are there not twelve hours in the day?
> If anyone walks in the day, he does not stumble, because he sees
> the light of this world. [10] But if anyone walks in the night, he stum-
> bles, because the light is not in him." [11] After saying these things,
> He said to them, "Our friend Lazarus has fallen asleep, but I go to

> awaken him." 12 The disciples said to Him, "Lord, if he has fallen
> asleep, he will recover." 13 Now Jesus had spoken of his death, but
> they thought that He meant taking rest in sleep. 14 Then Jesus told
> them plainly, "Lazarus has died, 15 and for your sake I am glad that
> I was not there, so that you may believe. But let us go to him." 16 So
> Thomas, called the Twin, said to his fellow disciples, "Let us also
> go, that we may die with Him."

1. Describe Jesus' relationship with this family (vv. 1–5). See also the passages below.

    > Now as they went on their way, Jesus entered a village. And a woman named Martha welcomed Him into her house. And she had a sister called Mary, who sat at the Lord's feet and listened to His teaching. But Martha was distracted with much serving. And she went up to Him and said, "Lord, do You not care that my sister has left me to serve alone? Tell her then to help me." But the Lord answered her, "Martha, Martha, you are anxious and troubled about many things, but one thing is necessary. Mary has chosen the good portion, which will not be taken away from her." (Luke 10:38–42)

    > Six days before the Passover, Jesus therefore came to Bethany, where Lazarus was, whom Jesus had raised from the dead. So they gave a dinner for Him there. Martha served, and Lazarus was one of those reclining with Him at table. Mary therefore took a pound of expensive ointment made from pure nard, and anointed the feet of Jesus and wiped His feet with her hair. The house was filled with the fragrance of the perfume. (John 12:1–3)

2. Why did Jesus purposely delay going to Bethany (vv. 6, 11–15)?

3. After His disciples object to going to Judea again (v. 8), what do you think Jesus means by His parable in response to them (vv. 9–10)?

4. What do the disciples fear (vv. 8, 16)?

READ JOHN 11:17–37.

> 17 Now when Jesus came, He found that Lazarus had already been
> in the tomb four days. 18 Bethany was near Jerusalem, about two
> miles off, 19 and many of the Jews had come to Martha and Mary
> to console them concerning their brother. 20 So when Martha
> heard that Jesus was coming, she went and met Him, but Mary
> remained seated in the house. 21 Martha said to Jesus, "Lord, if
> You had been here, my brother would not have died. 22 But even
> now I know that whatever You ask from God, God will give You."
> 23 Jesus said to her, "Your brother will rise again." 24 Martha said
> to Him, "I know that he will rise again in the resurrection on the
> last day." 25 Jesus said to her, "I am the resurrection and the life.
> Whoever believes in Me, though he die, yet shall he live, 26 and
> everyone who lives and believes in Me shall never die. Do you
> believe this?" 27 She said to Him, "Yes, Lord; I believe that You are
> the Christ, the Son of God, who is coming into the world."
>
> 28 When she had said this, she went and called her sister Mary,
> saying in private, "The Teacher is here and is calling for you."
> 29 And when she heard it, she rose quickly and went to Him.
> 30 Now Jesus had not yet come into the village, but was still in the
> place where Martha had met Him. 31 When the Jews who were
> with her in the house, consoling her, saw Mary rise quickly and
> go out, they followed her, supposing that she was going to the
> tomb to weep there. 32 Now when Mary came to where Jesus was

> and saw Him, she fell at His feet, saying to Him, "Lord, if You had
> been here, my brother would not have died." 33 When Jesus saw
> her weeping, and the Jews who had come with her also weeping,
> He was deeply moved in His spirit and greatly troubled. 34 And
> He said, "Where have you laid him?" They said to Him, "Lord,
> come and see." 35 Jesus wept. 36 So the Jews said, "See how He loved
> him!" 37 But some of them said, "Could not He who opened the
> eyes of the blind man also have kept this man from dying?"

5. Why does John mention that Lazarus had been in the tomb four days?

6. Where is Bethany (John 11:18)? How does this explain the disciples' concerns?

7. What does Martha's statement in verse 21 imply? How might she have felt, since Jesus did not come when they sent for Him?

8. What do you think she means in verse 22?

9. What else do you learn about Martha from her conversation with Jesus in verses 21–27? Have you ever felt that God was ignoring your cries for help?

10. What teaching on the resurrection might she have known? See Daniel 12:1–2 and John 5:28–29.

11. How does Jesus' claim in verses 25–26 stretch Martha's faith?

12. How is Martha's statement in verse 27, "I believe that You are the Christ, the Son of God, who is coming into the world," a powerful example to us?

13. When Mary came to Jesus, she repeated the same statement as Martha (v. 32). The two sisters had probably said this to themselves repeatedly.

a. How might this have contributed to Jesus' weeping and emotional response, even though He knew He was going to raise Lazarus to life (vv. 33–35)?

b. How can this account of Jesus weeping help you trust Him more?

14. Why did the mourners comment as they did in verses 36–37?

READ JOHN 11:38–44—JESUS RAISES LAZARUS.

> 38 Then Jesus, deeply moved again, came to the tomb. It was a cave,
> and a stone lay against it. 39 Jesus said, "Take away the stone." Mar-
> tha, the sister of the dead man, said to Him, "Lord, by this time
> there will be an odor, for he has been dead four days." 40 Jesus said
> to her, "Did I not tell you that if you believed you would see the
> glory of God?" 41 So they took away the stone. And Jesus lifted up
> His eyes and said, "Father, I thank You that You have heard Me.
> 42 I knew that You always hear Me, but I said this on account of
> the people standing around, that they may believe that You sent
> Me." 43 When He had said these things, He cried out with a loud
> voice, "Lazarus, come out." 44 The man who had died came out, his
> hands and feet bound with linen strips, and his face wrapped with
> a cloth. Jesus said to them, "Unbind him, and let him go."

15. Consider Martha's objection in verse 39. Contrast it with the confidence she voiced in verse 22.

16. How would you explain Jesus' words in verse 41, "I thank You that *You have heard Me*"?

17. What are the implications for us? Refer to John 15:15–17.

READ JOHN 11:45–57—THE PLOT TO KILL JESUS.

> 45 Many of the Jews therefore, who had come with Mary and had
> seen what He did, believed in Him, 46 but some of them went to
> the Pharisees and told them what Jesus had done. 47 So the chief
> priests and the Pharisees gathered the council and said, "What
> are we to do? For this man performs many signs. 48 If we let Him
> go on like this, everyone will believe in Him, and the Romans will
> come and take away both our place and our nation." 49 But one of
> them, Caiaphas, who was high priest that year, said to them, "You
> know nothing at all. 50 Nor do you understand that it is better for
> you that one man should die for the people, not that the whole
> nation should perish." 51 He did not say this of his own accord, but
> being high priest that year he prophesied that Jesus would die for
> the nation, 52 and not for the nation only, but also to gather into
> one the children of God who are scattered abroad. 53 So from that
> day on they made plans to put Him to death.
>
> 54 Jesus therefore no longer walked openly among the Jews, but
> went from there to the region near the wilderness, to a town
> called Ephraim, and there He stayed with the disciples.
>
> 55 Now the Passover of the Jews was at hand, and many went up
> from the country to Jerusalem before the Passover to purify them-
> selves. 56 They were looking for Jesus and saying to one another as
> they stood in the temple, "What do you think? That He will not
> come to the feast at all?" 57 Now the chief priests and the Pharisees

had given orders that if anyone knew where He was, he should let them know, so that they might arrest Him.

18. What are the different responses to this miracle? Why?

19. Consider the following thought questions:

    - Have you ever experienced a time when it felt like God was not answering your prayers? How did you deal with it?
    - Can you think of a time when you encountered a challenging situation that ended up stretching you and strengthening your faith? What might have been different for you if you had never experienced that difficulty? What is your testimony of God's provision in that circumstance?
    - How does your love for Jesus move you to action this week?

Closing Prayer and Blessing

The Triumphal Entry

And the crowds that went before Him and that followed Him were shouting, "Hosanna to the Son of David! Blessed is He who comes in the name of the Lord! Hosanna in the highest!" (Matthew 21:9)

Prayers

____

____

____

____

Read Matthew 21:1–11; Luke 19:37–44—Jesus Enters Jerusalem.

Matthew 21:1 Now when they drew near to Jerusalem and came to
Bethphage, to the Mount of Olives, then Jesus sent two disciples,
2 saying to them, "Go into the village in front of you, and immediately you will find a donkey tied, and a colt with her. Untie them
and bring them to Me. 3 If anyone says anything to you, you shall
say, 'The Lord needs them,' and he will send them at once." 4 This
took place to fulfill what was spoken by the prophet, saying,

5 "Say to the daughter of Zion, 'Behold, your king is coming to
you, humble, and mounted on a donkey, on a colt, the foal of a
beast of burden.'"

6 The disciples went and did as Jesus had directed them. 7 They
brought the donkey and the colt and put on them their cloaks,
and He sat on them. 8 Most of the crowd spread their cloaks on
the road, and others cut branches from the trees and spread them
on the road. 9 And the crowds that went before Him and that followed Him were shouting, "Hosanna to the Son of David! Blessed
is He who comes in the name of the Lord! Hosanna in the highest!" 10 And when He entered Jerusalem, the whole city was stirred
up, saying, "Who is this?" 11 And the crowds said, "This is the
prophet Jesus, from Nazareth of Galilee." . . .

Luke 19:37 As He was drawing near—already on the way down the
Mount of Olives—the whole multitude of His disciples began to

rejoice and praise God with a loud voice for all the mighty works
that they had seen, [38] saying, "Blessed is the King who comes in
the name of the Lord! Peace in heaven and glory in the highest!"
[39] And some of the Pharisees in the crowd said to Him, "Teacher,
rebuke Your disciples." [40] He answered, "I tell you, if these were
silent, the very stones would cry out."

[41] And when He drew near and saw the city, He wept over it, [42] saying, "Would that you, even you, had known on this day the things
that make for peace! But now they are hidden from your eyes.
[43] For the days will come upon you, when your enemies will set
up a barricade around you and surround you and hem you in on
every side [44] and tear you down to the ground, you and your children within you. And they will not leave one stone upon another
in you, because you did not know the time of your visitation."

1. How did Jesus demonstrate His identity as Messiah as He entered Jerusalem?

    a. See Matthew 21:2–3.

    b. See verses 6–7.

    c. See verse 9.

d. See Luke 19:41–44.

2. The greeting *hosanna* is a request for God to save us. *Hosanna* or "save us" is found in Psalm 118:25, a processional psalm praising God. By Jesus' time, the psalm had become part of the liturgical celebration of the Passover and Feast of Tabernacles. Read Psalm 118:24–28 to better understand how the processional shouts of hosanna fulfill messianic prophecy.

3. How might others have missed that Jesus was the Messiah?

4. Have you unexpectedly encountered God's presence in humble circumstances?

READ MATTHEW 21:12–17—JESUS CLEARS THE TEMPLE.

> 12 And Jesus entered the temple and drove out all who sold and
> bought in the temple, and He overturned the tables of the mon-
> ey-changers and the seats of those who sold pigeons. 13 He said to
> them, "It is written, 'My house shall be called a house of prayer,'
> but you make it a den of robbers."
>
> 14 And the blind and the lame came to Him in the temple, and
> He healed them. 15 But when the chief priests and the scribes saw
> the wonderful things that He did, and the children crying out in
> the temple, "Hosanna to the Son of David!" they were indignant,
> 16 and they said to Him, "Do You hear what these are saying?"
> And Jesus said to them, "Yes; have you never read, 'Out of the
> mouth of infants and nursing babies You have prepared praise'?"
>
> 17 And leaving them, He went out of the city to Bethany and
> lodged there.

5. Jesus ended His public ministry the way it began—by clearing the temple of money-changers and animal sellers. Jesus called the temple a "den of robbers," quoting Jeremiah 7:11. Read that passage and consider the historical events at Shiloh and Ephraim.

    a. What was significant about Shiloh and Ephraim?

b. What was Jesus telling the priests who came to rebuke Him for overturning the tables in the temple court of the Gentiles and for healing the blind and lame?

6. Matthew includes the accounts of Jesus healing the blind and lame at the temple and receiving hosannas from children as the fulfillment of additional messianic prophecies. Refer to Isaiah 35:4–6 and Psalm 8:1–2.

   What was the response of the chief priests and teachers of the law who knew the full context of the Scriptures being quoted?

7. After clearing the temple, Jesus began teaching about the kingdom of God through parables and illustrations in response to the Jewish religious leaders who demanded to know who gave Him the authority to cleanse the temple and teach in the temple courts. Through His illustrations of the kingdom of God, Jesus indicated that He was bringing the kingdom, but the Jewish leaders would not be a part of it. The parables were very much in contrast to the vision of Zion described by the prophets. The collection of parables makes a good study in themselves, but we only have time in this lesson to summarize their main points. Read as many as time permits and discuss the main points.

Parable or Illustration	Main Point
Matthew 21:18–22 The withered fig tree	The kingdom of heaven is given to those who produce fruit. Prayer and faith have extraordinary power.
Matthew 21:28–32 The two sons	Tax collectors and prostitutes are entering the kingdom of God ahead of the chief priests, elders, and teachers of the law in Israel because of their repentance and faith.
Matthew 21:33–44 The tenants	Since the Jewish religious leaders rejected Jesus, He will entrust His kingdom to the apostles, who will produce fruit.
Matthew 22:1–14 The wedding banquet	Those who reject God's invitation to enter His kingdom will be judged and destroyed.
Matthew 22:34–40 The greatest commandment	Love God with your heart, soul, and mind.
Mark 12:41–44 The widow's offering	God is pleased by joyful sacrifices of any size, not by large gifts from abundance.
Matthew 25:1–13 The ten virgins	The kingdom of heaven comes to those who prayerfully keep watch and await their Lord.
Matthew 25:14–30 The talents	Those who are given the kingdom of heaven produce the fruit of faith.
Matthew 25:31–46 The sheep and goats	The kingdom of heaven is given to those who demonstrate their faith by caring for the hungry, thirsty, poor, imprisoned, and stranger in need.

Based on the main points in Jesus' final parables, how would you define what Jesus meant by the kingdom of God (or kingdom of heaven)?

Closing Prayer and Blessing

The Lord's Supper

And He took bread, and when He had given thanks,
He broke it and gave it to them, saying, "This is My body,
which is given for you. Do this in remembrance of Me." (Luke 22:19)

Prayers

____

____

____

____

Background

1. How many sacraments are there in the following denominations? Circle the answer.

a. The Lutheran Church	0	2	7
b. The Roman Catholic Church	0	2	7
c. The Baptist Church	0	2	7

The seven sacraments in the Roman Catholic Church are Baptism, Eucharist, confirmation, penance, matrimony, orders, and extreme unction. The Lutheran Church recognizes two: Baptism and Communion.

2. There are three characteristics of a sacrament in the Lutheran Church. Fill in the blank.

   a. ________________ (commanded) by Jesus.

   b. For the __________________ of sin.

   c. Has a visible, tangible ____________.

3. The visible, tangible elements are these:

    a. Baptism—________.

    b. Communion—______ and ________.

4. Another name for Holy Communion is the Eucharist, from the Greek meaning ____________________.

5. (Multiple choice) The context for the first Lord's Supper when Christ instituted it was

    a. Passover

    b. Feast of Tabernacles

    c. Hanukkah

    d. Feast of Weeks (Pentecost)

6. True or false: Jesus celebrated the Passover many times, for many years, before He made the covenant of Communion in His body and blood.

7. Which of the following happens in Holy Communion?

    a. Jesus gives it as a gift; we are getting a specific gift from God!

    b. God grants forgiveness of sins for all who believe and receive.

    c. We receive abundant life and eternal salvation in Jesus Christ.

    d. We receive spiritual strength and victory over sin and Satan.

    e. God grants us grace and mercy.

    f. We proclaim the Lord's death and resurrection until He returns.

    g. We commune with God and with the members of the Body of Christ.

    h. All of the above.

8. (Fill in the blank) Lutherans believe the bread and wine are more than just symbolic because Jesus said, "This ____ My body. . . . This _____ My blood of the covenant, which is poured out for many for the forgiveness of sins" (Matthew 26:26, 28).

9. The word *sacrament* comes from the Latin word *sacramentum* for a sacred or solemn oath, but the original Greek word is *musterion* meaning ___________. Luther provided a profound insight into the mystery of the sacraments. Christ's body and blood are joined with the elements of bread and wine and the Holy Spirit is given to us with the element of water, but even more amazing is that God uses these elements for the forgiveness of sin, even for such a sinner as me.

10. Roman Catholics believe the bread and wine actually _________________ into the body and blood of Christ. Lutherans believe the body and blood of Christ are joined to the bread and wine.

READ LUKE 22:1–20.

> [1] Now the Feast of Unleavened Bread drew near, which is called
> the Passover. [2] And the chief priests and the scribes were seeking
> how to put Him to death, for they feared the people.
>
> [3] Then Satan entered into Judas called Iscariot, who was of the
> number of the twelve. [4] He went away and conferred with the
> chief priests and officers how he might betray Him to them. [5] And
> they were glad, and agreed to give him money. [6] So he consented
> and sought an opportunity to betray Him to them in the absence
> of a crowd.
>
> [7] Then came the day of Unleavened Bread, on which the Passover
> lamb had to be sacrificed. [8] So Jesus sent Peter and John, saying,
> "Go and prepare the Passover for us, that we may eat it." [9] They
> said to Him, "Where will You have us prepare it?" [10] He said to
> them, "Behold, when you have entered the city, a man carrying
> a jar of water will meet you. Follow him into the house that he
> enters [11] and tell the master of the house, 'The Teacher says to you,
> Where is the guest room, where I may eat the Passover with My
> disciples?' [12] And he will show you a large upper room furnished;
> prepare it there." [13] And they went and found it just as He had told
> them, and they prepared the Passover.
>
> [14] And when the hour came, He reclined at table, and the apostles
> with Him. [15] And He said to them, "I have earnestly desired to eat

> this Passover with you before I suffer. 16 For I tell you I will not eat it until it is fulfilled in the kingdom of God." 17 And He took a cup, and when He had given thanks He said, "Take this, and divide it among yourselves. 18 For I tell you that from now on I will not drink of the fruit of the vine until the kingdom of God comes." 19 And He took bread, and when He had given thanks, He broke it and gave it to them, saying, "This is My body, which is given for you. Do this in remembrance of Me." 20 And likewise the cup after they had eaten, saying, "This cup that is poured out for you is the new covenant in My blood."

1. What was the significance of Passover and the Passover Lamb? See Exodus 12:21–28.

> 21 Then Moses called all the elders of Israel and said to them, "Go and select lambs for yourselves according to your clans, and kill the Passover lamb. 22 Take a bunch of hyssop and dip it in the blood that is in the basin, and touch the lintel and the two doorposts with the blood that is in the basin. None of you shall go out of the door of his house until the morning. 23 For the LORD will pass through to strike the Egyptians, and when He sees the blood on the lintel and on the two doorposts, the LORD will pass over the door and will not allow the destroyer to enter your houses to strike you. 24 You shall observe this rite as a statute for you and for your sons forever. 25 And when you come to the land that the LORD will give you, as He has promised, you shall keep this service. 26 And when your children say to you, 'What do you mean by this service?' 27 you shall say, 'It is the sacrifice of the LORD's Passover, for He passed over the houses of the people of Israel in Egypt, when He struck the Egyptians but spared our houses.'" And the people bowed their heads and worshiped.
>
> 28 Then the people of Israel went and did so; as the LORD had commanded Moses and Aaron, so they did.

2. In light of the Passover in Jerusalem and Jesus' ministry, why were the priests and teachers so determined to kill Jesus?

3. Besides the desire to be with friends, why might Jesus "eagerly desire" to share this particular Passover feast with the disciples?

4. How will the Passover be fulfilled in the kingdom of God (Luke 22:16)?

5. How does Jesus' use of the bread and wine change the emphasis of Passover? What new meaning does He give to it?

6. Refer to the passages below and Exodus 12:21–28 to compare aspects of the old covenant and the new covenant Jesus brought.

Covenant Considerations

I. Compare blood in Exodus 12:21–28 (from question 1) to Romans 5:8–9.

II. Compare the act of remembrance in Passover from Exodus 12:21–28 to remembrance in Communion in 1 Corinthians 11:23–26.

III. Compare the role of a Jewish priest to Christ in Hebrews 10:11–18.

IV. Compare God's role in the salvation of His people in the old and new covenants found in Exodus 12:21–28 and John 3:16–17.

Elements of Sacrifice	Old Covenant	New Covenant
I. Blood	Sacrifice of animals for sin.	Jesus' blood, once for all.
II. Remembrance	Passover.	Communion.
III. Role of Priests in Sacrifice	Continually sacrificing for sin.	Jesus sacrifices Himself on the cross, once for all sin and for all mankind.
IV. God's Role in Salvation	God saved His people, the Israelites.	God's salvation is for all people.
V. The Role of Faith	By faith, the Israelites believed God would save them and deliver them from their enemies.	We are saved by faith in Jesus Christ.
VI. Forgiveness	Forgiveness under the law was through the daily sacrifice of animals.	Assurance of the forgiveness of sin is through faith that Jesus' blood has completely washed our sin away.

V. Compare the role of faith in the Passover celebration to Communion. Also compare Exodus 12:23–27 to John 3:16–17.

VI. Contrast forgiveness under the law to forgiveness under Christ. See Leviticus 9:7 and Matthew 26:26–29.

READ LUKE 22:21–30.

> [21] "But behold, the hand of him who betrays Me is with Me on the
> table. [22] For the Son of Man goes as it has been determined, but
> woe to that man by whom He is betrayed!" [23] And they began to
> question one another, which of them it could be who was going
> to do this.
>
> [24] A dispute also arose among them, as to which of them was to be
> regarded as the greatest. [25] And He said to them, "The kings of the
> Gentiles exercise lordship over them, and those in authority over
> them are called benefactors. [26] But not so with you. Rather, let the
> greatest among you become as the youngest, and the leader as one
> who serves. [27] For who is the greater, one who reclines at table or
> one who serves? Is it not the one who reclines at table? But I am
> among you as the one who serves.
>
> [28] "You are those who have stayed with Me in My trials, [29] and I
> assign to you, as My Father assigned to Me, a kingdom, [30] that you
> may eat and drink at My table in My kingdom and sit on thrones
> judging the twelve tribes of Israel."

7. How might the news of a betrayer have led to the argument about which of them was the greatest?

8. How did Jesus resolve that argument?

9. What does He mean by the promise in verses 28–30 to assign them a kingdom and to sit at His table?

10. What does sharing in the Lord's Supper mean to you?

11. What would it mean to apply Jesus' words about service (vv. 26–27) in your family life? work or neighborhood relationships? use of money/resources/time?

12. What makes it hard for you to apply this principle in those areas? What can help you do so?

Closing Prayer and Blessing

Final Instructions

I am the way, and the truth, and the life.
No one comes to the Father except through Me. (John 14:6)

Prayer

____

____

____

____

Background

On the night Jesus was betrayed, the Passover meal was prepared. Jesus eagerly desired to share this last meal with His disciples. He took a cup of wine, gave thanks, and announced that He would be betrayed. Then Jesus took the bread and the cup and instituted a new covenant of faith in His body and blood poured out for the forgiveness of sin. Judas left the table. The disciples questioned one another about who might be the betrayer and argued over who would be the greatest when Jesus came into His kingdom. Against this backdrop of betrayal and quarreling, Jesus began His final words of instruction, assurance, and comfort to His disciples. They are among the most familiar and beloved words in Scripture.

Read John 14:1–14.

> [1] "Let not your hearts be troubled. Believe in God; believe also
> in Me. [2] In My Father's house are many rooms. If it were not so,
> would I have told you that I go to prepare a place for you? [3] And
> if I go and prepare a place for you, I will come again and will take
> you to Myself, that where I am you may be also. [4] And you know
> the way to where I am going." [5] Thomas said to Him, "Lord, we
> do not know where You are going. How can we know the way?"
> [6] Jesus said to him, "I am the way, and the truth, and the life. No
> one comes to the Father except through Me. [7] If you had known
> Me, you would have known My Father also. From now on you do
> know Him and have seen Him."

> 8 Philip said to Him, "Lord, show us the Father, and it is enough for us." 9 Jesus said to him, "Have I been with you so long, and you still do not know Me, Philip? Whoever has seen Me has seen the Father. How can you say, 'Show us the Father'? 10 Do you not believe that I am in the Father and the Father is in Me? The words that I say to you I do not speak on My own authority, but the Father who dwells in Me does His works. 11 Believe Me that I am in the Father and the Father is in Me, or else believe on account of the works themselves.
>
> 12 "Truly, truly, I say to you, whoever believes in Me will also do the works that I do; and greater works than these will he do, because I am going to the Father. 13 Whatever you ask in My name, this I will do, that the Father may be glorified in the Son. 14 If you ask Me anything in My name, I will do it."

1. What does Jesus tell His disciples to believe about Himself and His relationship to God?

    a. Verses 1–4

    b. Verses 6–7

    c. Verses 9–11

d. Verses 12–14

2. In light of Jesus’ declaration that no one could come to God except through Him, how would you answer someone who thinks there are “many ways to God”?

Read John 14:15–31—Jesus Promises the Holy Spirit.

> 15 “If you love Me, you will keep My commandments. 16 And I will ask the Father, and He will give you another Helper, to be with you forever, 17 even the Spirit of truth, whom the world cannot receive, because it neither sees Him nor knows Him. You know Him, for He dwells with you and will be in you.
>
> 18 “I will not leave you as orphans; I will come to you. 19 Yet a little while and the world will see Me no more, but you will see Me. Because I live, you also will live. 20 In that day you will know that I am in My Father, and you in Me, and I in you. 21 Whoever has My commandments and keeps them, he it is who loves Me. And he who loves Me will be loved by My Father, and I will love him and manifest Myself to him.” 22 Judas (not Iscariot) said to Him, “Lord, how is it that You will manifest Yourself to us, and not to the world?” 23 Jesus answered him, “If anyone loves Me, he will keep My word, and My Father will love him, and We will come to him and make Our home with him. 24 Whoever does not love Me does not keep My words. And the word that you hear is not Mine but the Father’s who sent Me.
>
> 25 “These things I have spoken to you while I am still with you. 26 But the Helper, the Holy Spirit, whom the Father will send in My name, He will teach you all things and bring to your remem-

brance all that I have said to you. [27] Peace I leave with you; My peace I give to you. Not as the world gives do I give to you. Let not your hearts be troubled, neither let them be afraid. [28] You heard Me say to you, 'I am going away, and I will come to you.' If you loved Me, you would have rejoiced, because I am going to the Father, for the Father is greater than I. [29] And now I have told you before it takes place, so that when it does take place you may believe. [30] I will no longer talk much with you, for the ruler of this world is coming. He has no claim on Me, [31] but I do as the Father has commanded Me, so that the world may know that I love the Father. Rise, let us go from here."

3. Jesus tells His disciples to keep His commandments and to love one another five times in His final encouragements (John 14:15, 23; 15:10, 12, 17). What promises does Jesus make with respect to their obedience (14:21)? What are the implications of Jesus' command to Christians who keep sinning without repentance?

4. What does Jesus teach His disciples about the Holy Spirit?

    a. Verses 15–17

    b. Verse 18

c. Verse 26–27

5. How can we, like Jesus, have peace, comfort, and even rejoicing in the face of suffering and death (v. 28)?

READ JOHN 15:1–17—TRUE VINE AND THE BRANCHES.

> 1 I am the true vine, and My Father is the vinedresser. 2 Every
> branch in Me that does not bear fruit He takes away, and every
> branch that does bear fruit He prunes, that it may bear more fruit.
> 3 Already you are clean because of the word that I have spoken
> to you. 4 Abide in Me, and I in you. As the branch cannot bear
> fruit by itself, unless it abides in the vine, neither can you, unless
> you abide in Me. 5 I am the vine; you are the branches. Whoever
> abides in Me and I in him, he it is that bears much fruit, for apart
> from Me you can do nothing. 6 If anyone does not abide in Me he
> is thrown away like a branch and withers; and the branches are
> gathered, thrown into the fire, and burned. 7 If you abide in Me,
> and My words abide in you, ask whatever you wish, and it will
> be done for you. 8 By this My Father is glorified, that you bear
> much fruit and so prove to be My disciples. 9 As the Father has
> loved Me, so have I loved you. Abide in My love. 10 If you keep My
> commandments, you will abide in My love, just as I have kept My
> Father's commandments and abide in His love. 11 These things I
> have spoken to you, that My joy may be in you, and that your joy
> may be full.
>
> 12 This is my commandment, that you love one another as I have
> loved you. 13 Greater love has no one than this, that someone lay

down his life for his friends. [14] You are My friends if you do what
I command you. [15] No longer do I call you servants, for the servant does not know what his master is doing; but I have called
you friends, for all that I have heard from My Father I have made
known to you. [16] You did not choose Me, but I chose you and appointed you that you should go and bear fruit and that your fruit
should abide, so that whatever you ask the Father in My name, He
may give it to you. [17] These things I command you, so that you will
love one another.

6. What is required of us to be fruitful disciples? Give personal examples of living out these illustrations.

   a. Verse 2

   b. Verses 3, 10

c. Verse 4

d. Verses 7–8

7. What is the warning to Christians whose lives are not characterized by moral living, obedience, prayer, and acts of loving others?

8. What does it mean to you to abide in Christ as the branch in the vine?

Jesus continued teaching on the Holy Spirit after warning His disciples they would be hated, thrown out of the synagogues, and killed because of their love for Him.

READ JOHN 15:26–27; 16:4–15.

> 26 But when the Helper comes, whom I will send to you from the Father, the Spirit of truth, who proceeds from the Father, He will bear witness about Me. 27 And you also will bear witness, because you have been with Me from the beginning. . . .
>
> 16:4 I did not say these things to you from the beginning, because I was with you. 5 But now I am going to Him who sent Me, and none of you asks Me, "Where are You going?" 6 But because I have said these things to you, sorrow has filled your heart. 7 Nevertheless, I tell you the truth: it is to your advantage that I go away, for if I do not go away, the Helper will not come to you. But if I go, I will send Him to you. 8 And when He comes, He will convict the world concerning sin and righteousness and judgment: 9 concerning sin, because they do not believe in Me; 10 concerning righteousness, because I go to the Father, and you will see Me no longer; 11 concerning judgment, because the ruler of this world is judged.
>
> 12 I still have many things to say to you, but you cannot bear them now. 13 When the Spirit of truth comes, He will guide you into all the truth, for He will not speak on His own authority, but whatever He hears He will speak, and He will declare to you the things that are to come. 14 He will glorify Me, for He will take what is Mine and declare it to you. 15 All that the Father has is Mine; therefore I said that He will take what is Mine and declare it to you.

9. What is the Holy Spirit's role during times of persecution and trials (John 15:26; 16:13–15)?

10. What are some other works of the Spirit in the world (vv. 8–11)?

11. On your own, read through the rest of John 16 and 17. Which verses bring you comfort in these chapters?

Closing Prayer and Blessing

Redeemed! The Crucifixion

And Jesus said, "Father, forgive them,
for they know not what they do." (Luke 23:34)

Prayers

____

____

____

____

Background

What setting do you picture when you think of Jesus in glory?

a. In heaven with the Father calling the universe into existence?

b. As the Son of Man before the Ancient of Days (Daniel 7:13)?

c. A mighty warrior whose name is "the Word of God" and "the King of kings" leading the armies of heaven in the last days?

d. Shining bright on the mountaintop during the transfiguration?

e. Doing a mighty work like healing the sick, walking on water during the storm, or raising Lazarus from the dead?

All these are powerful images of Jesus in glory, and there are many others. I am reminded of these as I go to the Communion rail to partake of Jesus' blood and body, and I am reminded that we are in His kingdom *now* with His Spirit of love, power, and forgiveness abiding in us.

The day after Jesus' arrest, while it was still early in the morning, Jesus was again questioned by Caiaphas, the council of elders, chief priests, and teachers of the law. Jesus again confessed that He was the Son of God and was condemned to death. After Judas saw that Jesus was condemned by the Sanhedrin, he was seized with remorse. Judas returned the thirty pieces of silver, confessed his sin, and was told by the priests that it was not their concern. He went away to hang himself.

Jesus was taken to Pilate for questioning and sentencing in a Roman court because the Sanhedrin had no authority to carry out a death sentence. Read the account of Jesus' trial before Pilate in merged passages from John, Luke, and Matthew.

READ SELECTED VERSES FROM MATTHEW, LUKE, AND JOHN—JESUS BEFORE PILATE.

> John 18:28 Then they led Jesus from the house of Caiaphas to the gov-
> ernor's headquarters. It was early morning. They themselves did
> not enter the governor's headquarters, so that they would not be
> defiled, but could eat the Passover. 29 So Pilate went outside to
> them and said, "What accusation do you bring against this man?"
> 30 They answered him, "If this man were not doing evil, we would
> not have delivered Him over to you." 31 Pilate said to them, "Take
> Him yourselves and judge Him by your own law." The Jews said
> to him, "It is not lawful for us to put anyone to death." 32 This was
> to fulfill the word that Jesus had spoken to show by what kind of
> death He was going to die. . . .
>
> Luke 23:2 And they began to accuse Him, saying, "We found this man
> misleading our nation and forbidding us to give tribute to Caesar,
> and saying that He Himself is Christ, a king." . . .
>
> John 18:33 So Pilate entered his headquarters again and called Jesus
> and said to Him, "Are You the King of the Jews?" 34 Jesus an-
> swered, "Do you say this of your own accord, or did others say
> it to you about Me?" 35 Pilate answered, "Am I a Jew? Your own
> nation and the chief priests have delivered You over to me. What
> have You done?" 36 Jesus answered, "My kingdom is not of this
> world. If My kingdom were of this world, My servants would have
> been fighting, that I might not be delivered over to the Jews. But
> My kingdom is not from the world." 37 Then Pilate said to Him,
> "So You are a king?" Jesus answered, "You say that I am a king. For
> this purpose I was born and for this purpose I have come into the
> world—to bear witness to the truth. Everyone who is of the truth
> listens to My voice." 38 Pilate said to Him, "What is truth?" After
> he had said this, he went back outside to the Jews and told them,
> "I find no guilt in Him." . . .
>
> Matthew 27:12 But when He [Jesus] was accused by the chief priests and
> elders, He gave no answer. 13 Then Pilate said to Him, "Do You not
> hear how many things they testify against You?" 14 But He gave
> him no answer, not even to a single charge, so that the governor
> was greatly amazed. . . .

Luke 23:6 When Pilate heard this, he asked whether the man was a Galilean. 7 And when he learned that He belonged to Herod's jurisdiction, he sent Him over to Herod, who was himself in Jerusalem at that time. 8 When Herod saw Jesus, he was very glad, for he had long desired to see Him, because he had heard about Him, and he was hoping to see some sign done by Him. 9 So he questioned Him at some length, but He made no answer. 10 The chief priests and the scribes stood by, vehemently accusing Him. 11 And Herod with his soldiers treated Him with contempt and mocked Him. Then, arraying Him in splendid clothing, he sent Him back to Pilate. 12 And Herod and Pilate became friends with each other that very day, for before this they had been at enmity with each other.

13 Pilate then called together the chief priests and the rulers and the people, 14 and said to them, "You brought me this man as one who was misleading the people. And after examining Him before you, behold, I did not find this man guilty of any of your charges against Him. 15 Neither did Herod, for he sent Him back to us. Look, nothing deserving death has been done by Him. 16 I will therefore punish and release Him. . . .

John 18:39 "But you have a custom that I should release one man for you at the Passover. So do you want me to release to you the King of the Jews?" . . .

Matthew 27:18 For he knew that it was out of envy that they had delivered Him up. 19 Besides, while he was sitting on the judgment seat, his wife sent word to him, "Have nothing to do with that righteous man, for I have suffered much because of Him today in a dream." 20 Now the chief priests and the elders persuaded the crowd to ask for Barabbas and destroy Jesus. . . .

Luke 23:18 But they all cried out together, "Away with this man, and release to us Barabbas"— 19 a man who had been thrown into prison for an insurrection started in the city and for murder. 20 Pilate addressed them once more, desiring to release Jesus,

21 but they kept shouting, "Crucify, crucify Him!" 22 A third time he said to them, "Why? What evil has He done? I have found in Him no guilt deserving death. I will therefore punish and release Him." 23 But they were urgent, demanding with loud cries that He should be crucified. And their voices prevailed. . . .

Matthew 27:23 And he [Pilate] said, "Why? What evil has He done?" But they shouted all the more, "Let Him be crucified!"

24 So when Pilate saw that he was gaining nothing, but rather that

a riot was beginning, he took water and washed his hands before the crowd, saying, "I am innocent of this man's blood; see to it yourselves." [25] And all the people answered, "His blood be on us and on our children!" [26] Then he released for them Barabbas, and having scourged Jesus, delivered Him to be crucified.

1. Why did Pilate dismiss the Jewish leaders without hearing the charge against Jesus (John 18:29–31)? See also Matthew 27:18 and Mark 15:10.

2. What charge did the Jewish leaders bring against Jesus (Luke 23:2)?

3. Why did Pilate dismiss Jesus' admission that He was a king in the first round of questioning (John 18:33–38)?

4. What was Herod's hope in questioning Jesus (Luke 23:8)?

5. Why did Jesus refuse to answer any more questions from the chief priests, Pilate, or Herod?

Read Matthew 27:27–30; John 19:4–16—Jesus' Sentencing and Flogging.

Matthew 27:27 Then the soldiers of the governor took Jesus into the

> governor's headquarters, and they gathered the whole battalion before Him. 28 And they stripped Him and put a scarlet robe on Him, 29 and twisting together a crown of thorns, they put it on His head and put a reed in His right hand. And kneeling before Him, they mocked Him, saying, "Hail, King of the Jews!" 30 And they spit on Him and took the reed and struck Him on the head. And when they had mocked Him, they stripped Him of the robe and put His own clothes on Him and led Him away to crucify Him. . . .
>
> John 19:4 Pilate went out again and said to them, "See, I am bringing Him out to you that you may know that I find no guilt in Him." 5 So Jesus came out, wearing the crown of thorns and the purple robe. Pilate said to them, "Behold the man!" 6 When the chief priests and the officers saw Him, they cried out, "Crucify Him, crucify Him!" Pilate said to them, "Take Him yourselves and crucify Him, for I find no guilt in Him." 7 The Jews answered him, "We have a law, and according to that law He ought to die because He has made Himself the Son of God." 8 When Pilate heard this statement, he was even more afraid. 9 He entered his headquarters again and said to Jesus, "Where are You from?" But Jesus gave him no answer. 10 So Pilate said to Him, "You will not speak to me? Do You not know that I have authority to release You and authority to crucify You?" 11 Jesus answered him, "You would have no authority over Me at all unless it had been given you from above. Therefore he who delivered Me over to you has the greater sin."
>
> 12 From then on Pilate sought to release Him, but the Jews cried out, "If you release this man, you are not Caesar's friend. Everyone who makes himself a king opposes Caesar." 13 So when Pilate heard these words, he brought Jesus out and sat down on the judgment seat at a place called The Stone Pavement, and in Aramaic Gabbatha. 14 Now it was the day of Preparation of the Passover. It was about the sixth hour. He said to the Jews, "Behold your King!" 15 They cried out, "Away with Him, away with Him, crucify Him!" Pilate said to them, "Shall I crucify your King?" The chief priests answered, "We have no king but Caesar." 16 So he delivered Him over to them to be crucified.

6. In John 19:8, the Jewish leaders finally admit they want Jesus to die because He claimed to be the Son of God. Why would Pilate pronounce the death sentence on Jesus even though he declared Jesus to be innocent at least three times through the trial?

7. Jesus' trial has been described as a paradox and deeply ironic. What are some of the paradoxes of the trial with respect to the following:

   a. Jesus was judged and condemned by man.

   b. Jesus was accused of subversion.

   c. Jesus was accused of blasphemy.

Read the Merged Chronological Account of the Crucifixion

One person read the Gospel verse; another person read the prophecy that is fulfilled (ignore the headings and read only the Scripture).

The Crucifixion	Prophecy
Mark 15:21 And they compelled a passerby, Simon of Cyrene, who was coming in from the country, the father of Alexander and Rufus, to carry His cross.	
Mark 15:22 And they brought Him [Jesus] to the place called Golgotha (which means Place of a Skull).	
Luke 23:27 And there followed Him a great multitude of the people and of women who were mourning and lamenting for Him.	
Luke 23:28 But turning to them Jesus said, "Daughters of Jerusalem, do not weep for Me, but weep for yourselves and for your children.	

Luke 23:29 For behold, the days are coming when they will say, 'Blessed are the barren and the wombs that never bore and the breasts that never nursed!'	
Luke 23:30 Then they will begin to say to the mountains, 'Fall on us,' and to the hills, 'Cover us.'	Hosea 10:8 The high places of Aven, the sin of Israel, shall be destroyed. Thorn and thistle shall grow up on their altars, and they shall say to the mountains, "Cover us," and to the hills, "Fall on us."
Luke 23:31 For if they do these things when the wood is green, what will happen when it is dry?"	Ezekiel 20:47 Say to the forest of the Negeb, Hear the word of the LORD: Thus says the Lord GOD, Behold, I will kindle a fire in you, and it shall devour every green tree in you and every dry tree. The blazing flame shall not be quenched, and all faces from south to north shall be scorched by it.
Luke 23:32 Two others, who were criminals, were led away to be put to death with Him. [33] And when they came to the place that is called The Skull, there they crucified Him, and the criminals, one on His right and one on His left.	Isaiah 53:12a Therefore I will divide Him a portion with the many, and He shall divide the spoil with the strong, because He poured out His soul to death and was numbered with the transgressors.
Mark 15:25 And it was the third hour when they crucified Him.	Psalm 22:16 For dogs encompass Me; a company of evildoers encircles Me; they have pierced My hands and feet.
Luke 23:34a And Jesus said, "Father, forgive them, for they know not what they do."	Isaiah 53:12b Yet He bore the sin of many, and makes intercession for the transgressors.
Luke 23:34b And they cast lots to divide His garments.	Psalm 22:18 They divide My garments among them, and for My clothing they cast lots.
Luke 23:35 And the people stood by, watching, but the rulers scoffed at Him, saying, "He saved others; let Him save Himself, if He is the Christ of God, His Chosen One!"	Psalm 22:7 All who see Me mock Me; they make mouths at Me; they wag their heads; [8] "He trusts in the LORD; let Him deliver Him; let Him rescue Him, for He delights in Him!"
Luke 23:36 The soldiers also mocked Him, coming up and offering Him sour wine [mixed with myrrh but He did not take it] [37] and saying, "If You are the King of the Jews, save Yourself!"	

John 19:19 Pilate also wrote an inscription and put it on the cross. It read, "Jesus of Nazareth, the King of the Jews."	Matthew 2:1 Behold, wise men from the east came to Jerusalem, [2] saying, "Where is He who has been born king of the Jews? For we saw His star when it rose and have come to worship Him."
John 19:20 Many of the Jews read this inscription, for the place where Jesus was crucified was near the city, and it was written in Aramaic, in Latin, and in Greek.	
John 19:21 So the chief priests of the Jews said to Pilate, "Do not write, 'The King of the Jews,' but rather, 'This man said, I am King of the Jews.'"	
John 19:22 Pilate answered, "What I have written I have written."	

8. Who was in control of Jesus' death?

    a. Pilate

    b. Jewish leaders

    c. Roman soldiers

    d. Other

9. Why did Jesus regard His death as His glory while speaking to His disciples in the Upper Room during their Last Supper (John 12:23; 13:31)?

10. What is the significance of each of the signs and wonders that accompanied Jesus' death?

    a. There is darkness (the sun was not shining) over the whole land from noon to 3:00 p.m. (Matthew 27:45; Mark 15:33; Luke 23:44).

b. The curtain of the temple is torn in two from top to bottom (Matthew 27:51).

c. An earthquake splits rocks (Matthew 27:51).

d. Tombs are opened and dead arise (Matthew 27:52–53). (Note that the dead testify to others in Jerusalem after Jesus' resurrection.)

Our relationship with God flows from Jesus' suffering, blood, and death as God's sacrificial Passover lamb, as described in the various aspects of Christian doctrine listed below.

Salvation—Romans 10:9

Substitution—Romans 5:8

Sanctification—1 John 1:7

Redemption—Ephesians 1:7

Baptism—Romans 6:4

Communion—1 Corinthians 11:25

Reconciliation—Colossians 1:20

Justification—Romans 5:9

Atonement—Romans 3:25

Adoption—Ephesians 2:13

Election—1 Peter 1:1–2

11. Based on the doctrines listed above, how would you summarize what Jesus did for you?

Closing Prayer and Blessing

Notes on the People at Golgotha (The Place of the Skull)

a. Simon of Cyrene (Mark 15:21): Simon was from Libya and was probably in Jerusalem for the Passover. He was a passerby forced to carry Jesus' cross. There is no specific prophecy relating to his action. Jews from Cyrene received the Holy Spirit at Pentecost (Acts 2:10) and were some of the earliest missionaries (Acts 11:20), so perhaps Simon witnessed to his brothers all that he had seen.

b. Soldiers (John 19:23)
The soldiers' cruelty fulfilled Scripture that the Messiah would be God's Suffering Servant. They would divide His garments (Psalm 22:18) and pierce His side so that we might be healed by His wounds (Isaiah 53:5).

c. Two other criminals (robbers) (Luke 23:32; Mark 15:27)
Crucifixion with other criminals fulfilled prophecy that the Messiah would be numbered with transgressors as He poured out His life (Isaiah 53:12).

d. A large number of mourners (Luke 23:27)

Mourners fulfilled prophecy. "I will turn your feasts into mourning and all your songs into lamentation; I will bring sackcloth on every waist and baldness on every head; I will make it like the mourning for an only son and the end of it like a bitter day" (Amos 8:10).

e. Jewish rulers (chief priests, teachers of the law, elders) and mockers (Luke 23:35; Matthew 27:41)

The Jewish rulers were there to see that their plot to murder Jesus was successful. Their spite, mockery, and insults were prophetic fulfillment of Psalm 22:6–8.

f. Jesus of Nazareth, King of the Jews, Son of God (Lamb of God) (John 19:19; Matthew 27:43)

The crucifixion of Christ was the Lord's will to make His life a guilt offering for the world.

g. Roman centurion (Matthew 27:54)

The Roman centurion testified that the natural signs and resurrection of the dead made it clear that Jesus was the Son of God.

h. Women (John 19:25; Matthew 27:56)

The women were at the crucifixion as they had been throughout Jesus' ministry. While the other disciples (except John) cowered in fear, the women stayed to witness the events. Jesus appeared to them first since they went to the tomb to attend to His burial.

- Mary, Jesus' mother
- Joanna, wife of Chuza, Herod's household manager
- Mary, wife of Clopas
- Mary Magdalene
- Mary, the mother of James and Joseph
- The mother of the sons of Zebedee (James and John)

i. Joseph of Arimathea and Nicodemus (John 19:38–39)

Joseph was a Pharisee who buried Jesus in his tomb, fulfilling Scripture that the Messiah would be buried in the tomb of a rich man (Isaiah 53:9). Nicodemus was also a Pharisee, the same one who came to Jesus at night in John 3.

The Resurrection

He is not here, for He has risen, as He said.
Come, see the place where He lay. (Matthew 28:6)

Prayers

____

____

____

____

Background

The account of Jesus' resurrection is told by Matthew, Mark, Luke, and John. Each writer includes events that occurred on resurrection Sunday, but no writer tells all the events. The writers do not contradict one another; they simply include different details. This is true in all the Gospel accounts, but since the account of Jesus' resurrection is fundamental to our Christian faith, it comes under the most criticism. Critics argue over the number of women, the number of angels, whether Roman guards were posted or not, and the number of people to whom Jesus appeared that morning.

Matthew includes details about women who were at the cross when Jesus died; among them were Mary Magdalene, Mary the mother of James and Joseph, and the mother of the sons of Zebedee (Jesus' disciples James and John). Mark included Salome and wrote that many other women had come up with Jesus to Jerusalem for the Passover. Luke included Joanna among the women and said there were others also.

Matthew includes the detail of an earthquake and an angel rolling the stone away from the tomb, encountering the women at the entrance of tomb, and inviting them to see the empty place where Jesus lay. Mark and Luke mention that the women encountered angels in the tomb. Was there one angel or two, or was one angel joined by the other from the entrance of the tomb? We don't know exactly, only that these brave women who came to minister to Jesus' body were blessed by God to be the first to learn He had risen from the grave. The angels direct the women to tell the disciples Jesus had risen! As they went to do this, Matthew tells us Jesus appeared to the women, but we don't know if all of them were present or only some of the group.

John's resurrection account begins with Mary Magdalene telling him and Peter that someone had taken Jesus' body from the tomb. They ran to the tomb and found it empty. While Mary stayed at the tomb, Jesus appeared to her and called her by name, so that she could recognize Him.

Matthew closes his resurrection account with the guards reporting what they had witnessed at the tomb.

Although the details of the resurrection vary, the proclamation of the Gospels is clear: Jesus has risen! He has risen indeed!

READ MATTHEW 27:62–28:7.

> 27:62 The next day, that is, after the day of Preparation, the chief priests and the Pharisees gathered before Pilate 63 and said, "Sir, we remember how that impostor said, while He was still alive, 'After three days I will rise.' 64 Therefore, order the tomb to be made secure until the third day, lest His disciples go and steal Him away and tell the people, 'He has risen from the dead,' and the last fraud will be worse than the first." 65 Pilate said to them, "You have a guard of soldiers. Go, make it as secure as you can." 66 So they went and made the tomb secure by sealing the stone and setting a guard.
>
> 28:1 Now after the Sabbath, toward the dawn of the first day of the week, Mary Magdalene and the other Mary went to see the tomb. 2 And behold, there was a great earthquake, for an angel of the Lord descended from heaven and came and rolled back the stone and sat on it. 3 His appearance was like lightning, and his clothing white as snow. 4 And for fear of him the guards trembled and became like dead men. 5 But the angel said to the women, "Do not be afraid, for I know that you seek Jesus who was crucified. 6 He is not here, for He has risen, as He said. Come, see the place where He lay. 7 Then go quickly and tell His disciples that He has risen from the dead, and behold, He is going before you to Galilee; there you will see Him. See, I have told you."

1. Why were the women at the tomb so early? See Luke 23:55–24:1.

2. What obstacles did they face at the tomb?

READ MATTHEW 28:8–10; JOHN 20:1–18.

> Matthew 28:8 So they [the women] departed quickly from the tomb with fear and great joy, and ran to tell His disciples. 9 And behold, Jesus met them and said, "Greetings!" And they came up and took hold of His feet and worshiped Him. 10 Then Jesus said to them, "Do not be afraid; go and tell My brothers to go to Galilee, and there they will see Me." . . .
>
> John 20:1 Now on the first day of the week Mary Magdalene came to the tomb early, while it was still dark, and saw that the stone had been taken away from the tomb. 2 So she ran and went to Simon Peter and the other disciple, the one whom Jesus loved, and said to them, "They have taken the Lord out of the tomb, and we do not know where they have laid Him." 3 So Peter went out with the other disciple, and they were going toward the tomb. 4 Both of them were running together, but the other disciple outran Peter and reached the tomb first. 5 And stooping to look in, he saw the linen cloths lying there, but he did not go in. 6 Then Simon Peter came, following him, and went into the tomb. He saw the linen cloths lying there, 7 and the face cloth, which had been on Jesus' head, not lying with the linen cloths but folded up in a place by itself. 8 Then the other disciple, who had reached the tomb first, also went in, and he saw and believed; 9 for as yet they did not understand the Scripture, that He must rise from the dead. 10 Then the disciples went back to their homes.
>
> 11 But Mary stood weeping outside the tomb, and as she wept she stooped to look into the tomb. 12 And she saw two angels in white, sitting where the body of Jesus had lain, one at the head and one at the feet. 13 They said to her, "Woman, why are you weeping?" She said to them, "They have taken away my Lord, and I do not know where they have laid Him." 14 Having said this, she turned around and saw Jesus standing, but she did not know that it was Jesus. 15 Jesus said to her, "Woman, why are you weeping? Whom are you seeking?" Supposing Him to be the gardener, she said to Him, "Sir, if You have carried Him away, tell me where You have laid Him, and I will take Him away." 16 Jesus said to her, "Mary." She turned and said to Him in Aramaic, "Rabboni!" (which means

> Teacher). [17] Jesus said to her, "Do not cling to Me, for I have not yet ascended to the Father; but go to My brothers and say to them, 'I am ascending to My Father and your Father, to My God and your God.'" [18] Mary Magdalene went and announced to the disciples, "I have seen the Lord"—and that He had said these things to her.

3. John identifies three witnesses at the empty tomb: Mary Magdalene, Peter, and the other disciple (John). What important details do we learn from each?

4. What is the significance of Jesus' appearing to the women before appearing to the other disciples?

5. Does anything surprise you about Mary's interaction with the angels?

6. What does her response say about her emotional state and why she didn't recognize Jesus?

7. After Mary realized it was Jesus, how did her whole demeanor change?

   How would you explain Jesus' words to her?

8. How does Jesus refer to His disciples (John 20:17)? What is new in their relationship (see John 15:15)?

9. In light of Matthew 4:10, what does it mean that the disciples worshiped Jesus?

READ MATTHEW 28:11–15—THE GUARDS' REPORT.

> [11] While they were going, behold, some of the guard went into the
> city and told the chief priests all that had taken place. [12] And when
> they had assembled with the elders and taken counsel, they gave
> a sufficient sum of money to the soldiers [13] and said, "Tell people,
> 'His disciples came by night and stole Him away while we were
> asleep.' [14] And if this comes to the governor's ears, we will satisfy
> him and keep you out of trouble." [15] So they took the money and
> did as they were directed. And this story has been spread among
> the Jews to this day.

10. How does the guards' report and the fact that Jesus appeared first to women help validate the truth about the resurrection in contrast to the account the Pharisees devised?

11. Why is it important to prove the tomb was empty? How are John's details significant?

12. On what evidence do you base your belief that Jesus rose from the dead?

13. Is believing that Jesus rose from the dead as important as believing He died on the cross to take our sins upon Himself? Why or why not?

14. Of all the miraculous signs John included in his account, which have been the most significant or convincing to you and why?

15. Mary Magdalene wanted to hold on to Jesus, but Jesus sent her on a mission to tell others He was alive. How is Jesus sending you and to whom? Ask God to give you an opportunity to share the Good News of Jesus with someone this week.

Closing Prayer and Blessing

Commissioning and Ascension

Thus it is written, that the Christ should suffer and on the third day rise from the dead, and that repentance for the forgiveness of sins should be proclaimed in His name to all nations, beginning from Jerusalem. You are witnesses of these things. (Luke 24:46–48)

Prayers

____

____

____

____

Background

Recall where we left off in the story of Jesus' resurrection—Jesus died, He was buried in a specific tomb, Pilate authorized guards and a seal, the women saw the empty tomb and the risen Jesus and told the disciples, and Peter and John saw the empty tomb.

Read Luke 24:13–35—On the Road to Emmaus.

> [13] That very day two of them were going to a village named Em-
> maus, about seven miles from Jerusalem, [14] and they were talking
> with each other about all these things that had happened. [15] While
> they were talking and discussing together, Jesus Himself drew near
> and went with them. [16] But their eyes were kept from recognizing
> Him. [17] And He said to them, "What is this conversation that you
> are holding with each other as you walk?" And they stood still,
> looking sad. [18] Then one of them, named Cleopas, answered Him,
> "Are You the only visitor to Jerusalem who does not know the
> things that have happened there in these days?" [19] And He said to
> them, "What things?" And they said to Him, "Concerning Jesus
> of Nazareth, a man who was a prophet mighty in deed and word
> before God and all the people, [20] and how our chief priests and
> rulers delivered Him up to be condemned to death, and crucified
> Him. [21] But we had hoped that He was the one to redeem Israel.

Yes, and besides all this, it is now the third day since these things happened. 22 Moreover, some women of our company amazed us. They were at the tomb early in the morning, 23 and when they did not find His body, they came back saying that they had even seen a vision of angels, who said that He was alive. 24 Some of those who were with us went to the tomb and found it just as the women had said, but Him they did not see." 25 And He said to them, "O foolish ones, and slow of heart to believe all that the prophets have spoken! 26 Was it not necessary that the Christ should suffer these things and enter into His glory?" 27 And beginning with Moses and all the Prophets, He interpreted to them in all the Scriptures the things concerning Himself.

28 So they drew near to the village to which they were going. He acted as if He were going farther, 29 but they urged Him strongly, saying, "Stay with us, for it is toward evening and the day is now far spent." So He went in to stay with them. 30 When He was at table with them, He took the bread and blessed and broke it and gave it to them. 31 And their eyes were opened, and they recognized Him. And He vanished from their sight. 32 They said to each other, "Did not our hearts burn within us while He talked to us on the road, while He opened to us the Scriptures?" 33 And they rose that same hour and returned to Jerusalem. And they found the eleven and those who were with them gathered together, 34 saying, "The Lord has risen indeed, and has appeared to Simon!" 35 Then they told what had happened on the road, and how He was known to them in the breaking of the bread.

1. Why did Jesus use the testimony of Scripture before revealing Himself?

2. See verse 21. Compare how the disciples expected Jesus to redeem Israel to God's plan of redemption.

Read Luke 24:36–53—The Ascension.

> 36 As they were talking about these things, Jesus Himself stood
> among them, and said to them, "Peace to you!" 37 But they were
> startled and frightened and thought they saw a spirit. 38 And He
> said to them, "Why are you troubled, and why do doubts arise in
> your hearts? 39 See My hands and My feet, that it is I Myself. Touch
> Me, and see. For a spirit does not have flesh and bones as you
> see that I have." 40 And when He had said this, He showed them
> His hands and His feet. 41 And while they still disbelieved for joy
> and were marveling, He said to them, "Have you anything here
> to eat?" 42 They gave Him a piece of broiled fish, 43 and He took it
> and ate before them.
>
> 44 Then He said to them, "These are My words that I spoke to you
> while I was still with you, that everything written about Me in the
> Law of Moses and the Prophets and the Psalms must be fulfilled."
> 45 Then He opened their minds to understand the Scriptures,
> 46 and said to them, "Thus it is written, that the Christ should suf-
> fer and on the third day rise from the dead, 47 and that repentance
> for the forgiveness of sins should be proclaimed in His name to all
> nations, beginning from Jerusalem. 48 You are witnesses of these
> things. 49 And behold, I am sending the promise of My Father
> upon you. But stay in the city until you are clothed with power
> from on high."
>
> 50 And He led them out as far as Bethany, and lifting up His hands
> He blessed them. 51 While He blessed them, He parted from them
> and was carried up into heaven. 52 And they worshiped Him and
> returned to Jerusalem with great joy, 53 and were continually in
> the temple blessing God.

3. How is "peace be with you" a good summary of the Gospel (see v. 36)?

4. In verses 37–43, how did Jesus help the disciples believe He was real and not an apparition?

5. See verse 44. What are some things Jesus might have revealed to the disciples about Himself through the Scriptures? Refer to the following verses from the Law of Moses, the Psalms, and the Prophets:

   The Law of Moses: The Law of Moses primarily focuses on the covenant promises God made to Abraham to make him into a great nation and to bless all nations through him. Jesus was the fulfillment of that promise. There are additional passages that relate to His death and suffering.

   a. Genesis 3:15

   b. Numbers 21:9

The Psalms

a. Psalm 22:1

b. Psalm 22:6–8

c. Psalm 22:16–18

d. Psalm 16:9–10

The Prophets

a. Isaiah 53:3–5

b. Isaiah 53:12

c. Zechariah 13:7

6. Return to Luke 24:46. Even though there are abundant references to the suffering and death of God's Anointed, why was it so difficult for the disciples to understand that the Christ would suffer, die, and rise from the dead on the third day?

7. Verse 47 summarizes Jesus' commission to His disciples to be His witnesses proclaiming repentance for the forgiveness of sins in Jesus' name to all nations. Matthew included Jesus' instructions to "make disciples of all nations, baptizing them in the name of the Father and of the Son and of the Holy Spirit, teaching them to observe all that I have commanded you" (Matthew 28:19–20). How is this seemingly impossible commission happening in our generation?

8. Jesus appeared first to the women who came to minister to His body at the tomb and then to His disciples over a period of forty days (Acts 1:3) until prior to Pentecost, when He sent the Holy Spirit to empower them. During this period of appearing to them, He offered convincing proofs that He was physically alive. What did the resurrection prove about Jesus?

9. In Luke 24:52, why is it significant that the Scriptures include that the disciples worshiped Jesus?

10. In light of your current circumstances, where is the mission field Jesus has sent you? Who are some of the people with whom you can share the Good News that God loves them and showed His love to them through His Son, Jesus?

Closing Prayer and Blessing

Now Jesus did many other signs in the presence of the disciples, which are not written in this book; but these are written so that you may believe that Jesus is the Christ, the Son of God, and that by believing you may have life in His name. (John 20:30–31)